The Royal Air Force 1939-1945

Chaz Bowyer

Pen & Sword Paperbacks
Barnsley

First published 1984 by Ian Allan
Published in 1996 by Pen & Sword Paperbacks
an imprint of Pen & Sword Books Limited
47 Church Street, Barnsley,
South Yorkshire S70 2AS

ISBN 0 85052 528 4

Copyright © Chaz Bowyer 1984, 1996

A CIP record of this book is available from the
British Library

Printed and bound in
Great Britain by
Redwood Books, Trowbridge, Wiltshire

Contents

Prologue

When, in 1939, the Royal Air Force girded its loins for war with Germany for the second time, it was very much a 'junior' Service when compared with the British Army and the Royal Navy, having only in that same year 'come of age' by celebrating its 21st 'birthday' on 1 April. Though young in years the 'Third Service' was certainly not lacking in traditions of loyalty, courage and superb devotion to duty; nor had those interim years 1919-39 been spent in idleness or lotus-eating. *Every* day of those 20 years of so-termed 'peace' had seen some element of the RAF engaged in operational warlike activities at one or more outposts of the British Empire or other areas of the globe; operations which were seldom publicised (even today) but which accumulatively claimed no small toll of RAF casualties. Yet for most of those years the RAF was much neglected by its political 'masters' — indeed, its very existence as a separate Service had been a bone of high contention between its brother fighting Services, and the RAF had been very much a 'Cinderella between two great Ugly Sisters' in terms of financial support and governmental comprehension of its huge potential significance.

For the first of those two decades the infant RAF, due solely to lack of adequate financing, had little option but to fulfil its many, varying duties with obsolete aircraft of 1917-18 vintage, and equally outdated equipment. At the Armistice of November 1918 it had been the world's first independent (of Army and Navy control) air service, and incidentally the largest in numerical context. Reduced to a tenth of that overall strength by 1920, the 'peacetime' RAF remained virtually static as far as firstline aircraft and armament were concerned until the early 1930s, when the first serious moves were implemented by governments to rearm and modernise the Service.

Though these 'expansion' plans continued to be modified from time to time, at least the basis of the future RAF was established, with plans for an eventual bombing force equipped with twin- and four-engined truly heavy bombers, and a metropolitan fighter defence to receive modern eight-gun monoplane designs. The other prime operational aspect, epitomised by Coastal Command's role of protection of the UK's vital import shipping supply 'lines', still remained glue-footed in the context of up-dating, however — sufficient financial provisioning was still unprovided. Thus, when Britain and other European countries tottered on the very brink of all-out war with Nazi Germany in September 1938, it was a sobering fact that the RAF's operational strength and capabilities for engaging in any such conflict were, to put it mildly, 'doubtful' if not actually insignificant.

If their aircraft were patently outdated, or barely on a par with Luftwaffe counterparts then, the air and ground crews of the RAF were of high quality; thoroughly trained and deeply committed to their chosen professions. They were in the main products of Trenchard's visionary proposals 20 years before for 'his' air force; men nurtured at Cranwell, Halton, Cosford, Flowerdown and Eastchurch *et al* mingled with direct-entry 'regulars', and all steeped in RAF lore and tradition. Every man had been a volunteer on enlistment — the prewar RAF had no 'pressed men' in its ranks. On their shoulders fell the onus of responsibility for prosecuting the RAF's war during 1939-40 particularly, and thereafter leading and guiding the huge wartime influx of 'duration-only' airmen in RAF ways and means of waging war in the air. Inevitably, perhaps, such prewar stalwarts formed a high proportion of the Service's early casualties in France and the epic Battle of Britain in 1939-40; men whose inculcated experience was to be sorely missed until wartime-trained men could fill the 'gaps'. Fortunately, many of the latter quickly proved to be of equal quality and prowess, and even embellished the reputation of their forebears.

Of the RAF's actual operational efforts throughout the war, the following chapters and statistics will, I hope, give ample evidence. Certainly, my overall intention in this book has been to provide a ready reference form of war record for the RAF during the fateful years 1939-45. Naturally, it would be impossible to include literally every facet and statistic of such a gigantic subject within the necessarily limited parameters of one slim volume. However, I have attempted, at least, to present the skeleton framework, with some of the more important 'flesh and bones' attached here and there. Equally, certain sections of this book have been included in the hope of recreating the authentic 'atmosphere' of those years. A third purpose in compilation has been hopefully to dispel the occasional myth or legend so firmly believed still by latter-day students, historians, and would-be authors of the overall subject. Perhaps now — a forlorn hope admittedly — writers and broadcasters will no longer refer to 'hangers' when they mean hangars, or aircraftsmen when the 'gen' title is aircraftman, etc.

One aspect should be emphasised. War is not glamorous, despite the efforts of novelists and Hollywood film writers to present it as such. Life in the RAF during 1939-45 certainly had no 'glamour'; for the vast majority of men and women who served in RAF 'blue' it was a period of deprivation, separation from kith and kin, too often barely civilised living and working conditions, routine drudgery. For those men serving on a regular engagement it may have been a vocational life, a readily accepted epitome of their *raison d'être* as 'defenders of the realm'; but to many wartime-enlisted men and women their 'war' was a period of hazard and, more usually, boredom and frustration. There were, of course, 'high' spots too — comradeship, occasional 'triumphs' over daunting circumstances, and the ever present morale-sustaining esoteric brand of RAF 'twisted' humour. Indeed, any summary of RAF life then might be contained in that classic RAF saying — 'If you can't take a joke, you shouldn't have joined' . . .

Chaz Bowyer
Norwich 1996

RAF Command Structures and Organisation 1939-45

As a monarchy the United Kingdom of Great Britain has always invested ultimate command authority in its reigning sovereign. In 1939-45 this was HM King George VI, who held the ranks of Marshal of the Royal Air Force and Air Commodore-in-Chief, Auxiliary Air Force; both ranks in his particular case dating from 11 December 1936. To assist the King in RAF matters he had, in 1939, a Personal Aide-de-Camp (AVM HRH The Duke of Gloucester), a Principal Air Aide-de-Camp (ACM Sir Hugh C. T. Dowding), and two Air Aides-de-Camp (Grp Capt D. F. Stevenson and The Hon R. A. Cochrane). Immediately subordinate to HM The King was the Air Council, which in November 1939 comprised:

President
  Secretary of State for Air (Sir Kingsley Wood, MP)
Vice-President
  Parliamentary Under-Secretary of State for Air (Capt H. H. Balfour)
Members
  Chief of the Air Staff (ACM Sir Cyril Newall)
  Air Member for Personnel (AM C. F. A. Portal)
  Air Member for Development & Production (AM Sir Wilfrid R. Freeman)
  Air Member for Supply & Organisation (AM W. L. Welsh)
  Deputy Chief of the Air Staff (AM R. E. C. Peirse)
  Director-General of Production (E. J. H. Lemon)
  Additional Member (Sir Harold G. Howitt)
  Permanent Under-Secretary of State for Air (Sir Arthur Street)

Each Air Member controlled a department of the Air Ministry, divided into various specific directorates appropriate to his appointment

title; while the remainder of the Air Ministry was segmented into particular directorates, departments, committees, *et al*, all manned primarily by members of the Civil Service. Within Air Ministry aegis in late 1939 were also such 'sections' as the Royal Aircraft Establishment, Farnborough; Civil Aviation; Judge Advocate General of the Forces; Air Attaches to foreign Embassies and Legations; and Inspectors General of the RAF.

The next levels of authority in descending order from the Air Ministry were RAF Commands, each (normally) being commanded by an Air Officer Commanding-in-Chief (AOC-in-C). At the outbreak of war in 1939 these Commands were:

Command	AOC-in-C
Bomber Command:	ACM Sir Edgar Ludlow-Hewitt
Fighter Command:	ACM Sir Hugh C. T. Dowding
Coastal Command:	AM Sir Frederick W. Bowhill
Training Command:	AM Sir Arthur Longmore
Maintenance Command:	AVM J. S. T. Bradley
Balloon Command:	AVM O. T. Boyd
Reserve Command:	ACM Sir John M. Steel
RAF Middle East:	AM Sir William G. S. Mitchell
Air Forces in India:	AM Sir John F. A. Higgins
RAF Palestine & Trans-Jordan:	Air Cdre J. H. D'Albiac*
RAF in Iraq:	AVM J. H. S. Tyssen*
RAF Mediterranean:	Air Cdre R. Leckie*
RAF Aden	AVM G. R. M. Reid*
RAF Far East	AVM J. T. Babington*

The overseas Commands marked * were commanded by an Air Officer Commanding only (AOC) in September 1939.

Each UK-based Command was sub-divided into Groups for administrative convenience and, often, operational or non-operational roles. In September 1939 these were:

Bomber Command HQ

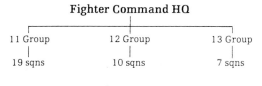

1 Group	2 Group	3 Group	4 Group	5 Group	6 Group
10 sqns	7 sqns	8 sqns	6 sqns	8 sqns	16 sqns (Training)

Fighter Command HQ

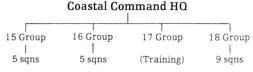

11 Group	12 Group	13 Group
19 sqns	10 sqns	7 sqns

Coastal Command HQ

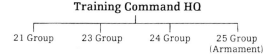

15 Group	16 Group	17 Group	18 Group
5 sqns	5 sqns	(Training)	9 sqns

Training Command HQ

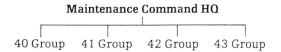

21 Group	23 Group	24 Group	25 Group (Armament)

Maintenance Command HQ

40 Group	41 Group	42 Group	43 Group

Reserve Command HQ

50 Group (Training)	51 Group (Training)	54 Group (Training)

Balloon Command HQ

30 Group	31 Group	32 Group	33 Group

Each Group was commanded by an officer of Air Rank ie Air Commodore or (more usually) Air Vice-Marshal.

In September 1939, with only two exceptions, all overseas Commands, being much smaller in strength than any UK-based Command, were sub-divided into Wings at most, thus:

RAF Middle East

RAF Iraq	RAF Aden	RAF Mediterranean	RAF Palestine & Trans-Jordan
1 Sqn	3 sqns	1 sqn	1 sqn

Egypt Group	252 Wing	Sudan Wing
10 sqns	2 sqns	2 sqns

Air Forces in India

1 (Indian) Group	2 sqns	Indian Air Force
4 sqns		1 sqn

RAF Far East

9 sqns

1
ACM Sir Cyril Newall, Chief of Air Staff 1937-40.
Faher

As the war progressed the RAF expanded swiftly, flexibly, to meet each change in operational and non-operational necessities, resulting in many changes in unit and higher organisational titlings, apart from the creation of often temporary formations for specific roles or other exigencies which later disbanded or were absorbed into existing formations. Equally, unit strengths and paper establishments for personnel and aircraft or other equipment varied from time to time, resulting in a number of rapid, if temporary, promotions at most rank levels to retain the necessary levels of Service authorisation and responsibility. Thus, from about 1941 it was quite usual to find squadrons commanded by Wing Commanders, flights within squadrons commanded by Squadron Leaders, and wings commanded by Group Captains etc. Even within the non-commissioned rank levels, as units began to expand or be newly created from 1940 onwards, junior NCOs were often promoted 'on the spot' to senior NCO and even

2
ACM Sir Edgar Ludlow-Hewitt, AOC-in-C, Bomber Command 1937-40.

3
The Air Council in session, Air Ministry, March 1941. L-R: Capt Harold Balfour MC, MP, Parliamentary Under Secretary of State for Air; Rt Hon Sir Archibald Sinclair Bt, PC, CMG, MP, Secretary of State for Air; ACM Sir Charles Portal, Chief of the Air Staff, 1940-45. *British Official*

Warrant Officer ranks to fill fresh establishments.

The extent of that RAF expansion may be judged by the state of the organisational structure in early 1945. In summary:

Unit	No of Groups	
Bomber Command	13	–
Fighter Command	7	
Coastal Command	7	(plus Iceland and Gibraltar)
Flying Training Command	7	
Tech Training Command	4	
Maintenance Command	4	
Transport Command	4	
2nd Tactical Air Force	4	
Balloon Command	1	
RAF, Northern Ireland	—	

Overseas
Middle East (inc Balkan AF, East Africa, Iraq, Aden, etc)
   8 Groups, 23 Wings, 3 other formations
SEAC (ACSEA)
   10 Groups, 4 Wings, 2 Elements in other Task Forces

In the United Kingdom the sheer acreage occupied by the RAF (and from 1942 the USAAF) was staggering. In 1939 the RAF could count almost 170 airfields under its control, though a huge construction programme was already well under way which eventually built no less than 444 during 1939-45 alone, apart from myriad extensions of main runways *et al*, and at least 20 more flying boat bases/stations around the UK's coastlines. By 1945, by including commandeered civil airports, satellite landing grounds, etc, the RAF could boast a total of nearly 700 'airfields' on UK territory alone. These foregoing figures related only to actual airfields having runways, be these grass or concrete. What they do not include are the literally hundreds of 'non-flying' stations in the UK — training schools for non-flying ground crews, signals and radar units, administrative centres, maintenance units (MUs), storage depots, and many other RAF-controlled locations.

At station level internal organisation was usually on a three-wing basis, ie Flying (where appropriate), Technical, and Administration; each (normally) commanded by a Wing Commander. Each wing was further sub-divided

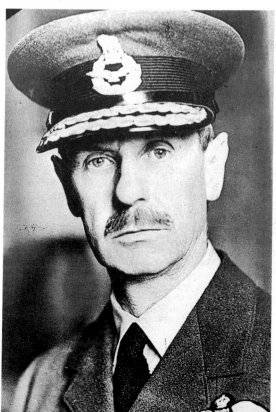

4
ACM Sir Hugh Dowding, AOC-in-C, Fighter Command, 1936-40.

5
ACM Sir Frederick Bowhill, AOC-in-C, Coastal Command, 1937-41.

into squadrons, flights and sections, each of these having at least a nominal 'Officer Commanding' (OC), though these were often junior officers, Warrant Officers, or occasionally a senior NCO. Station routine was promulgated in the form of Daily Routine Orders (DROs) from Station Headquarters (SHQ), though despite their title DROs were usually issued weekly rather than daily. These DROs gave full details of such routine matters as station duties (Orderly Officer, Orderly Sergeant, duty personnel, etc), parades, changes of responsibilities, and the hundred and one other items incurred in daily working practices. DROs were posted on notice boards in every section, flight and squadron office — and ignorance of any DRO (as with many other published rules or regulations) was *never* acceptable by 'higher authority' as an excuse for failure to comply with same! Station security was primarily a matter for the Service Police (SP), but many stations mounted a nightly guard comprising detailed airmen and junior NCOs — a duty neither loved nor welcomed by most airmen, being additional to their normal trade duties and work. Individual 'security' was manifested by the possession of a Service Identity Card (Form 1250) which bore a small passport-type photograph of the holder, apart from Service number, name, and contemporary rank — a card officially required to be carried on the person at *all* times.

Accommodation on every station might vary enormously, from the relative luxury of a prewar constructed station with proper barrack blocks and individual Officers' and Sergeants' Messes etc, to the nondescript collection of wooden and corrugated Nissen huts which constituted 'home' on most wartime-built airfields. Most stations had a NAAFI (Navy, Army & Air Force Institute) canteen, or a similar canteen provided by such organisations as the Salvation Army ('Sally Ann' in air-men's slang) or Church Army *et al*, to provide light refreshments, sweets and chocolate (on strict ration basis), etc, and often facilities for music, indoor games, or simply 'quiet rooms' for those preferring a modicum of peace and quiet after the long working day. Visiting entertainments occurred from time to time, by such organisations as ENSA ('Every Night Something Awful' in airmen's jargon ...), the main (but not the only) national association of professional show business people. All transport and airmen/airwomen entering or leaving an RAF station were required (officially ...) to do so via the station guardroom, located just inside the main gate entrance, and were 'booked' in or out by the duty personnel there. The guardroom housed not only the station Service Police offices but also the station's detention cells for miscreants, and was the venue for defaulters' parades (Jankers), station guards, etc.

Postings of all personnel from one unit to another originated ultimately from the RAF Records Office, including postings to overseas' Commands, but most Commands, particularly those outside the United Kingdom, usually authorised purely 'internal' postings of personnel, and then formally notified the Records Office of same in order to up-date documentation records. Personnel about to be posted to an overseas Command were placed on the PWR (Preliminary Warning Roll) and notified by Records Office, thereby permitting an airman to proceed on embarkation leave prior to actually leaving the UK; at least, that was the official procedure if time permitted. In practice many airmen were given only the briefest of 'preliminary warning', and 'embarkation leave' (if indeed any ...) could consist of merely a 48-hours' leave pass; the 'exigencies of the Service', especially in wartime, took small account of individual domestic considerations.

Secretaries of State for Air, 1939-45

Rt Hon Sir Kingsley Wood MP:	From 16 May 1938
Rt Hon Sir Samuel J. G. Hoare Bt, GCSI, CBE, CMG, MP:	5 April 1940
Rt Hon Sir Archibald Sinclair Bt, KT, CMG, MP:	11 May 1940
Rt Hon Harold Macmillan MP:	28 May 1945
Rt Hon Viscount Stansgate DSO, DFC:	3 August 1945

Chiefs of the Air Staff

ACM Sir Cyril Newall GCB, CMG, CBE, AM:	From 1 September 1937
ACM Sir Charles Portal GCB, DSO, MC	25 October 1940
ACM Sir Arthur Tedder GCB	1 January 1946

Squadrons

Notwithstanding the vast technical, administrative, and other 'internal' organisations of the RAF, all such facets have as their ultimate purpose the constant support and efficiency of the Service's 'sharp end' — the operational units which bear the prime responsibility for implementing the RAF's defensive and offensive capabilities. The foremost operational unit has always been the squadron, a unit of aircraft, air crews, and airmen ostensibly 'self-contained' in its ability to become mobile at short notice, and therefore able to be utilised as a 'single' operational unit should the need arise. The actual establishment of men and machines on any individual firstline squadron varied throughout 1939-45 for a variety of practical reasons. Fighter squadrons varied in

6
Spitfire Vb, AA842 of 349 (Belgian) Sqn, displaying typical unit codings and markings for late 1943 period.

aircraft (and thereby, personnel, air and ground) from 12 to 16 to 24 machines according to which stage of the war is considered. Bomber squadrons steadily increased from a peacetime establishment framed around 12 aircraft of twin-engined design with crews of (at most) four men, to 24 or even more four-engined aircraft with crews of seven or eight men. In Coastal Command most firstline squadrons, initially equipped mainly with flying boats but later embracing land-based 'heavies' such as the American Consolidated B-24 Liberator, usually had far less numbers of actual aircraft per squadron. Nevertheless, many of these aircraft not only carried larger crews — up to 10 men on certain designs — but often carried 'spare' crew men, air and ground, to cope with the fatigues and physical stresses of operational patrols lasting 12, 16, 18 or even longer hours.

Three squadrons initially constituted a wing, though this number varied between two and five squadrons at certain periods. Each squadron had its own commanding officer, initially a Squadron Leader from the peacetime RAF establishment, but more usually a Wing Commander from 1940 onwards; while wings came to be commanded by Group Captains, and groups by Air Commodores and Air Vice-Marshals as the war progressed and the Service expanded rapidly. Within a squadron were at least three operational flights, commonly titled A, B, and C, plus a small administrative 'HQ' flight; though the latter quickly disappeared from use where — as was the usual case — squadrons were based at established RAF stations possessing all the necessary support organisations. At the outbreak of war all squadrons had their own unit ground crews for maintenance of first-line servicing of unit aircraft, and major servicing repairs *et al*, ie tasks beyond the capability of a

7

Original members of the first American 'Eagle' squadron (No 71, RAF) at Kirton-in-Lindsey, Lincs on 8 April 1941.

1-299:	RAF
300-309:	Polish
310-315:	Czechoslovak
316-318:	Polish
320-322:	Dutch
326-329:	Free French
330-334:	Norwegian
335-336:	Greek
340-347:	Free French
349-350:	Belgian
351-352:	Yugoslav
353-358:	RAF India
400-445:	RCAF
450-467:	RAAF
485-490:	RNZAF
500-504:	Ex-AAF
510-539:	RAF Special Duties
540-544:	RAF PR
547-550:	RAF
567-598:	RAF
600-616:	Ex-AAF
617-750:	RAF
561-662:	RAF AOP
663:	Polish
664-666:	RCAF AOP
667-679:	RAF
680-684:	RAF PR
691-695:	RAF
900-947:	RAF Balloon
1435:	RAF

squadron's actual resources, were undertaken by base station personnel or even maintenance units (MUs). By the end of the war, however, many squadrons no longer 'possessed' esoteric ground crews, these being officially posted to Squadron Servicing Echelons 'attached' to particular squadrons; the Echelons normally incorporating the squadron number in its 'legal' title eg 6074 Servicing Echelon 'attached' to No 74 Squadron.

All squadrons of the RAF were allotted official numbers as their official title; most of those numbered from 1 to 274 having originally inherited their title from their Royal Flying Corps or Royal Navy Air Service forebears of 1912-18. During 1939-45 the huge expansion in strength of the RAF created numerous fresh squadrons and officialdom accordingly allocated 'blocks' of numbers to squadrons to cover specific roles, origins, *et al*, including the many Commonwealth and other 'non-British' units which ultimately operated under RAF control. As the war circumstances and operational situations changed from time to time, some squadrons were disbanded and/ or either become retitled or disappeared from the frontline strength; thus not all squadrons necessarily existed at the same moment in time. The overall official allotment of numbers for squadrons during 1939-45 were:

Several points should be emphasised regarding the above allocation 'blocks'. Not every number came to be used, while several squadrons tasked with specific or specialised roles were not solely within the particular 'block' indicated here: eg Nos 138 and 161 Squadrons RAF became Special Duties squadrons during the war. Though nominally RAF, Nos 71, 121 and 133 Squadrons were initially formed as the American Eagle squadrons and remained so until their US personnel were transferred to the USAAF in September 1942.

The two blocks allotted to ex-Auxiliary Air Force squadrons need a note of clarification. At the outbreak of war in 1939 the AAF mobilised a total of 20 squadrons; 14 of these within Fighter Command, and the other six with Coastal Command or Army Co-operation. On 3 September 1939, while still retaining their county/city titlings, all AAF personnel were officially 'transferred' to the RAF Volunteer Reserve (RAFVR) for the 'duration of hostilities'. Nevertheless, AAF personnel continued to distinguish themselves from RAFVR men by wearing a pair of small brass 'A'

8
Pilots of 609 Squadron at Manston, early 1943 proudly display their unit badge outside their dispersal hut. *Imperial War Museum(IWM)*

9
Wg Cdr I. R. Gleed DSO, DFC, Wing Leader of the Ibsley Wing (Nos 118, 234 and 501 Sqns), 1942, in front of Spitfire Vb, AA742 bearing his personal 'initials' code letters. *Dr D. L. Gleed*

badges on their uniform tunic jacket lapels. The Auxiliary Air Force was not reconstituted *per se* until 2 June 1946, and on 16 December 1947, in recognition of the superb wartime record of AAF units and personnel, HM King George VI assented to the addition of a royal prefix, thereby 'creating' the Royal Auxiliary Air Force.

Although each squadron under RAF control was primarily specified and distinguished by its official number, individual identification was also allocated by a system of code letters painted along the fuselage flanks of their aircraft. These, basically, were applied as two-letter codings to denote a particular squadron or unit followed by a third letter to indicate individual aircraft within each squadron or unit. The original introduction of the two-letter codings came via an Air Ministry Order (AMO) A.154/39, dated 27 April 1939, in respect of existing and projected squadrons at that time — an aftermath of the September 1938 'Munich Crisis'. On 4 September 1939, however, all such codings were completely changed in the interests of security, with only five known squadrons continuing to employ their prewar codes in the war period. As the war continued, a myriad of variations and additions to the code-letter system, soon used by virtually every form of flying unit both

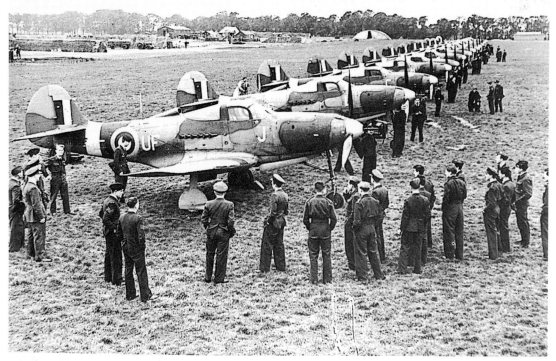

10
Auxiliaries. No 601 Sqn's Bell Airacobra fighters
lined up in 1941, bearing the unit's code-letters UF.
Sport & General Agency

operational and non-operational, came into
being. Similar code-letter combinations
appeared in certain squadrons based in the UK
and some overseas war zones; this being permitted since confusion could not occur within
either zone itself. In early 1941 Fighter
Command introduced the role of Wing Leader,
an operational 'Master of Ceremonies' who
controlled fighter formations in combat. To
help his subordinates to distinguish the
Leader's aircraft, Wing Leaders were granted
the privilege of using the initials of their name
as their individual codings: eg AGM was
Adolph Gysbert ('Sailor') Malan, and DB belong
to Douglas Bader — the latter emphasising his
private code letters by adopting his R/T call-
sign 'Dog's Body'.

In normal circumstances a squadron
operated as a single entity, albeit in conjunction with other squadrons within the aegis
of its particular wing; but it became fairly
common practice at certain stages of the war
for individual flights of a squadron to be
detached from the squadron base and operate
separately at some other airfield to meet
specific operational needs. These detached
flights should not be confused with more than
1,000 flights actually formed and numbered as
individual units for particular roles. The latter
flights were 'complete' units in their own right,
but were not sufficiently large enough in
established numbers of aircraft and personnel
to 'qualify' for full squadron status. One exception only was No 1435 Flight which was
formed on Malta in 1941 as a fighter flight,
flying Hurricanes in defence of the island. By
mid-1942 the flight had expanded sufficiently
to become retitled No 1435 Squadron with
effect from 2 August 1942 — the only four-
figure numbered *squadron* of the RAF, which
finally disbanded on 29 April 1945.

14

Ground Crews

Despite the age-old Service joke that certain airmen had not so much a 'trade' as a 'disease', eg Service Police or Physical Training Instructors, *all* airmen and airwomen enlisted in the RAF and WAAF were allotted to a specific trade within the overall trade structure. Basically, there were six trade groups, Nos I to V, and M. These groups reflected the degree of technical skill and responsibility within certain standard RAF trades, ie whether a top skilled fitter, a mechanic with no engineering training, or non-technical tasks. Accordingly, the most skilled tradesmen were those mustered in Group I, descending in levels of skill and basic training requirements to Group V — the latter including newly-joined recruits — while Group M represented mainly medical or nursing categories. Daily rates of basic pay for all ranks below commissioned officer varied at each rank level according to which trade Group the individual was mustered in; eg a Corporal in Group I had a basic daily pay rate of 7/6d, whereas a Corporal in trade Group V received a basic daily pay rate of 4/6d. This pay range may be illustrated by the following table which indicates the minimum and maximum daily basic pay rates, from AC2 to Warrant Officer, by trade group:

Group I   3/9d to 16/6d
Group II: 3/6d to 15/-
Group III: 3/- to 13/6d
Group IV: 3/3d to 14/-
Group V: 2/- to 13/6d
Group M: 2/- to 13/6d

These were *basic* pay rates, calculated on a daily basis, but additional payments were made in individual cases for various reasons. For example, certain specialist qualifications directly relevant to some trades could bring the holder extra payment of 'non-substantive' daily 'bonus' pay varying from 3d to 1s. All airmen and airwomen having a service record of very good conduct were also awarded 3d per day additional to basic rate at each stage of completing three, eight, and 13 years such service in the RAF.

Throughout the war the three lowest grades of non-commissioned airmen and airwomen, ie AC2/ACW2, AC1/ACW1, and LAC/LACW were not holders of *rank*, in the strict Service definition of holding general, if limited, powers of discipline over subordinates. These were instead trade classifications, denoting the holder's current standing according to successful trade testing results, eg to attain the LAC/LACW's coveted propellers' arm badge meant passing all facets of the appropriate trade

11
Installing an oxygen bottle in a Hurricane, 1940. Note each Erk is carrying his issue gas mask — mandatory dress then.

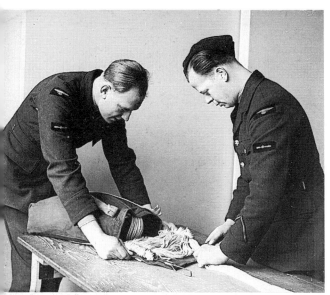

12
Parachute-packing at Ringway, early 1941. The LAC (rt) has one Good Conduct 'stripe' on his lower sleeve, denoting three years' completed service. *British Official*

13
Muscle-power. LAC J. Holland and Cpl L. Lott about to load a 250lb GP/HE bomb under the wing of Hurricane II 'Q-Queenie' of 402 Sqn RCAF at Warmwell, 9 February 1942. *Public Archives of Canada*

14
Never too old . . . AC1 L. H. Pakenham-Walsh, a Link Trainer Instructor who was born 1893, served in the RFC 1917-18, winning a DFC and French *Croix de Guerre* and retiring from RAF as a Flight Lieutenant in 1922, but re-enlisted as an Erk 1942-45.

Boys in the $15\frac{1}{2}$ to 17 years' age range could still enlist as a 'Trenchard Brat' via competitive and medical examinations, but actual entries were restricted to two per year, each limited to 300 vacancies, and the traditional three year apprenticeship training course was reduced to two years. It remained the *only* method of becoming an RAF 'regular' throughout the war years, and apprentices were trained at Halton (for most trades) and Cranwell (wireless trade). In February 1945, however, the 'peacetime'

15
Cpl 'Fergie' Ferguson (rt) supervising refuelling of a 57 Sqn Lancaster at East Kirkby.
Sqn Ldr H. B. Mackinnon, DFC

testing examinations at a minimum 80% pass mark. Therefore it will be seen that the lowest true *rank* was Corporal. Actual promotion from LAC/LACW to Corporal or higher ranks depended upon many things, including establishment vacancies, 'seniority' at existing level of rank or classification, recommendation initially by unit commander, etc, etc. Overall authority for such promotion rested ultimately with the RAF Records Office, which authority also issued air postings' notifications, confirmation of substantive rank promotions, and myriad other facets of RAF life affecting all ranks. On a local level, unit and station commanders had limited powers of authority to promote individuals to temporary higher rank in order to fill a key vacancy in unit/station organisation, but such temporary rank would be removed on the individual's eventual posting to another unit, unless confirmed by RAF Records Office in the interim, or the lack of a vacancy for such a rank at the new unit.

The vast bulk of wartime enlistments in the RAF and WAAF, including officers and air crews, were not members of the 'regular' RAF but were enlisted in the RAF Volunteer Reserve (RAFVR). At the beginning of the war all forms of entry to RAF regular service were temporarily halted, including the Boy Entrant scheme and the Cranwell College Cadetship course, with the single exception of the Aircraft Apprenticeship scheme. This latter 'breeding ground' for future RAF 'regulars' continued throughout the war without interruption, albeit on a reduced scale to the prewar standards.

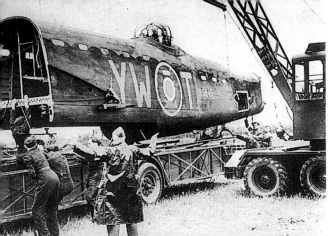

16
Fuselage of crashed Lancaster R5845 of 1660 HCU (ex-97 Sqn) being lowered by Coles Crane on to trailer of a 'Queen Mary' transporter for transit to an MU. *Keystone Agency*

17
Replenishing the oxygen supply of Mosquito 'W' of 613 Sqn, Lasham, 1944. *Flight International*

18
Sand-boys. Erks of No 1 Armoured Car Company RAF in the Western Desert, 1942. *E. Cant*

standard three-year course recommenced at Halton, while at Cranwell the Cadet course restarted from October 1946 in slightly extended form to the prewar two-year syllabus.

The generic slang term for all non-commissioned airmen below the rank of Corporal was 'Erks' — a term applied over many years before, during and, indeed, after the 1939-45 war, and one used with almost a degree of affection in everyday RAF language; whereas the official term was 'Other Ranks', a term commonly resented. Even more resented among the RAF 'minions' was the oft-used term inherited from the Army, and used by unthinking junior officers, of 'Troops'. A further common irritation to any ex-airman or serving Erk is/was the misspelling of Aircraftman/Aircraftwoman, by the insertion of an 's' between 'aircraft' and 'man/woman'. Put at its simplest explanation, an AC was an aircraftman, *not* an air-craftsman. This misunderstanding of the Erk's basic descriptive title continues to be prevalent . . .

Once enlisted, an airman's 'terms of service' during the war were relatively vague, beyond the certain knowledge that he was unlikely to be released from the Service until the close of the war unless for medical reasons, or other individual possibilities. He automatically became subject to all and every rule and regulation to be found in KRs and ACIs, was bound in disciplinary matters by the imposing volume MAFL, apart from a host of temporary wartime impositions placed upon all Servicemen and civilians. He could be (and often was) posted at the shortest of notices to far-flung corners of the globe, with no redress. If such a posting was to an overseas theatre of operations, his stay outside his homeland was undefined in the context of specific length of sojourn, ie there were no laid-down, set parameters to an overseas' tour of duty. This might be mere months, or (more often) two, three or even four years away from kith and kin, with no known date for repatriation to his homeland until only weeks before actually leaving his unit abroad. Even 'working hours' depended on myriad considerations on whichever particular unit, station, or Command he might be on or in. Traditionally (then) no Serviceman could belong to a trades union, hence his working life became a simple matter of 'Service exigencies' — a term sufficiently vague enough to 'cover' all of any imposed working structure.

19
Allotted bed-space and 'furnishings' for an airman at West Malling. Note three 'biscuit' mattresses stacked under the blankets.

20
Be it ever so 'umble . . . 'home' for LAC Jock Nicol, a Glaswegian, in the squadron Armoury. *Illustrated*

Working hours — the fetish of modern trades union officialdom — varied sharply, but generally depended to a great extent upon an airman's trade, and especially whether he was serving with a frontline operational unit, or employed in non-combatant areas and other facets of service. The usual working week for Erks on operational stations was at least six and a half days of 'labouring' at their individual trades, with a 48-hours' pass about

21
Just one of the various organisations which served the RAF — in this case at West Malling, 1945-46.

22
DI — Daily Inspection of Mosquito FBVI of 613 Sqn under way. Note ubiquitous Fordson tractor in foreground. *Flight International*

once per month, and very occasionally a few days' leave — IF 'exigencies' permitted, of course. For the ground crews directly concerned with the aircraft, however, these worked whenever work was necessary, even if this meant staying on the job until the task was completed, day and/or night. In support of the 'spanner brigade' toiling out on bleak dispersals or in draughty, unheated hangars, were the cooks, clerks, equipment, pay and MT, etc, etc — each equally important in the overall 'teamwork'. If the 'vitality' of certain apparently mundane duties rather escaped those involved, without their back-up the organisation might have crumbled rapidly.

Inevitably, the air crews, representing the 'sharp end' of the RAF's *raison d'etre*, received the lion's share of media publicity, awards and honours; inheriting an aura of 'glamour' in the lay eye. Yet to place just one pilot in one aeroplane and get both airborne has always needed a host of non-flying back-up, essential services. Put bluntly, without such support all air crews become immediately redundant. Fortunately on most, if not all, operational units the unstinting labours and devotion to duty of the unglamorous Erks were genuinely appreciated by the air crews, thereby forging an efficient, mutually co-operating team. Only as one 'progressed' further back from frontline operations did the gap open up between the 'leaders' and the 'led', widening overtly as that 'range' increased . . . 'Press on rewardless' might well have been sanctified as most Erks' official motto . . . !

23
Mobile flying control 'wagon' at Lasham, early 1944. *Flight*

24
Having completed all pre-flight inspections, an Erk gets the pilot's 'autograph' in the aircraft's individual Form 700 (Aircraft Servicing Log) before entrusting 'his' aircraft to the air crew. *Flight*

Training

At the beginning of the war the RAF controlled all training, air and ground, within a single Training Command, a formation which itself had been inaugurated in 1936 during the Service's general reorganisation in that year. Command HQ then was at Market Drayton, but moved to Shinfield Park, Reading, in January 1940. Then, on 28 May 1940, Training Command *per se* was officially disbanded and replaced by separate Commands to control Technical Training and Flying Training. The latter Command at that time controlled 80 training schools — 31 of these being devoted to pilot training — and had an establishment of 3,189 aircraft of 56 different types. HQ Flying Training Command remained at Shinfield Park; while Technical Training Command HQ became situated nearby at Wantage Hall, where it remained until shortly after the end of the war.

Flying Training

Prior to the outbreak of war RAF pilots received almost 150 flying hours' instruction and practice before being posted to squadrons, where they underwent further 'continuation' training until considered fully competent to undertake normal squadron flying duties. Once squadrons were mobilised for their wartime roles, however, they had no facilities or personnel to spare to 'polish' newly-trained pilots, and this final stage was undertaken on Group Pool or Reserve squadrons initially, ie units relegated to training duties within each group. By 1941 such advanced training units became titled Operational Training Units (OTUs). Hence, the progress of any would-be pilot now became eight weeks ground instruction at an Initial Training Wing (ITW); 10 weeks of flying and ground lessons at an Elementary Flying Training School (EFTS); followed by up to 16 weeks at a Service Flying Training School (SFTS) on 'advanced' flying practice; then on to an OTU for a final 4-6 weeks getting used to the type of aircraft they would actually be flying on operations with their designated squadron. Overall, pilots therefore received some 200 flying hours in their log books before commencing operational duties. Later in the war, in the case of bomber pilots in particular, the training sequence expanded slightly to include spells of instruction at additional stages, eg Heavy Conversion Units (HCUs), and, if posted on to Lancasters, a Lancaster Finishing School (LFS); this raised the number of logged flying hours to as much as 350-360 before commencing squadron operations.

With the huge influx of recruits for air crew training, especially in 1939-40 initially, many completed their training up to OTU stage outside the United Kingdom — mainly under the aegis of the Empire Air Training Scheme —

25
The RAF's basic trainer throughout 1939-45 was the De Havilland Tiger ('Tiggy') Moth two-seater.

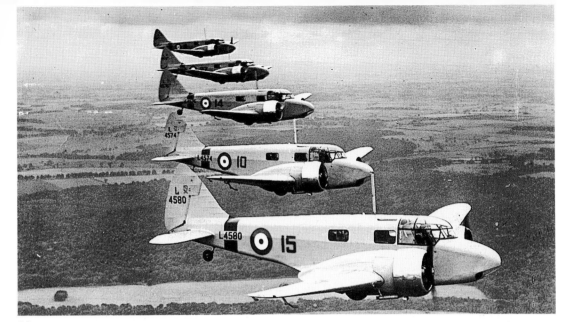

26
Those crews destined for multi-engined operational units received initial experience in the Airspeed Oxford.

in such countries as Canada, the USA and Kenya, the first EATS students reaching the UK in November 1940. All OTUs were controlled within the operational Commands to which the trainees were ultimately to be posted. When a bomber pilot reached the OTU stage he normally 'gathered' his future crew here within the first 48 hours from assembled navigators, bomb-aimers, wireless operators and air gunners — a procedure left entirely to the crews to select their own future operational companions. Once agreed, such crews then (theoretically at least) remained together and trained as a crew at the OTU, then joined their squadron together. It was then normal practice, if circumstances permitted, for the pilot to fly several actual operations as 'deputy'

27
The 'Maggie', or Miles Magister trainer.

to an experienced operational pilot, before
eventually captaining his own crew on sorties
over enemy territory.

The complete evolution process from raw
recruit to qualified pilot and commencement of
a first tour of operations varied at certain
stages of the war, due primarily to the fluctuat-
ing needs for particular categories of air crew
personnel, and not uncommonly stretched over
two or even more years. Conversely, many
crews at the OTU stage were detailed for
actual operations when any particular
'maximum effort' was mounted, especially the
bomber crews.

Technical Training (Ground trades)

Throughout 1939-45 almost two million men
and women served in the RAF at some stage of
the war, of which some 70% were enlisted in
non-flying trades — an indication in itself of
the massive supportive organisation necessary

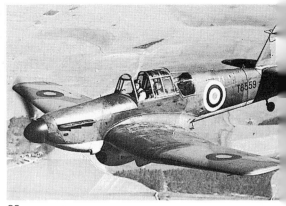

28
The Miles Master offered high-speed experience to
embryo fighter pilots.

29
In overseas theatres training was equally
prodigious. This Tiger Moth at Risalpur, India in
1940 was one of the batch of civil aircraft
'commandeered' from eight flying clubs throughout
India in 1939-40 for RAF use.

30
Modern aircraft trainers were seldom available
overseas. This Hawker Audax, K7525, saw service
with No 4 FTS, Abu Sueir, Egypt. *T. F. W. Addis*

31
The doughty Avro Anson gave long and faithful service in myriad roles. This example belonged to No 33 SFTS, Carberry, Manitoba in Canada; seen here in early 1943 on a cross-country training flight. *L. Pilgrim DFC*

32
Getting the Gen. Future airframe mechanics studying an aircraft hydraulic brake system at an RAF Technical Training School, 1941.
British Official

to maintain the RAF's operational flying 'sharp end'. Just prior to the outbreak of war RAF manning numbered less than 120,000, all ranks, but mobilisation and the huge number of volunteers for war service presented the training facilities with unprecedented problems of accommodation, training equipment, etc. Though eventually possessing 175 training units, the RAF was quickly forced to utilise a variety of alternative civilian facilities. Pure billeting was solved to a large degree by the use of traditional seaside hotels at such holiday centres as Blackpool, Morecambe, Torquay, etc; while venues for conversion to training workshops for technical tradesmen and women were aided by the 'Garage Scheme', whereby civilian garages became mechanical trades' instruction centres. Elsewhere, for specialised technical trades such as signals, radar, *et al*, the General Post Office (GPO), British Broadcasting Corporation (BBC) and several universities provided facilities and even instructors to cope with the increasing flood of trainees.

The bulk of wartime technical tradesmen were not skilled fitters in the accepted RAF definition for its Group I tradesmen, but mechanics trained in the 'ironmongery' applicable to their trade without any general engineering 'background' training. As the upper age limits for initial enlistment rose during 1941-45, however, many new recruits were already qualified tradesmen to civilian standards, and these were often absorbed into the Service with only minimal training. The skilled fitters of each Group I trade were, in the main, prewar or wartime regular Servicemen; a high proportion of these (initially at least) being ex-Aircraft Apprentices from Halton and Cranwell, and ex-Boy Entrants who had remustered via a fitters' course of instruction to become fitters. Other regular tradesmen 'serving their time' had often enlisted originally in lower Group trades, then by dint of experience and further training courses gradually risen in technical status to the highest Group. Attainment of the coveted LAC 'props' in any lower Group trade did not mean permanent retention of that status; entry to a more skilled trade Group meant having to 'earn' fresh status by means of successful trade testing results.

In all, more than 350 trades or sub-trades had to be catered for by the end of the war as the technical facets of the RAF became more complex. Apart from the fairly common 8-12 weeks' initial drill and 'bull' course suffered by all new recruits, the length of trade training courses — the next step for each recruit — varied from a few weeks for unskilled trades to 18-24 months for the more skilled branches. In the case of men commissioned in any ground technical trade these came from, basically, two major 'sources'; ex-SNCOs on regular service,

33
A much-used 'twin' trainer for the Empire Air Training Scheme was the Cessna Crane 1a (AT-17A) in Canada.

34
The future RAF. HM King George VI inspecting Cranwell Cadets on 13 June 1945. Each Cadet wears the white 'u/t Aircrew' flash in his hat.

35
Father and Sons. MRAF Lord Trenchard inspecting Aircraft Apprentices at Halton, 1945. Behind the 'Father of the RAF' a distinguished 'retinue' includes ACM Portal, CAS, AM Arthur Barratt (AOC, Technical Training Command), and (immediately behind Trenchard) Air Cdre H. G. White, AOC Halton.

36
The Fount. No 1 School of Technical Training, Halton, Bucks. In foreground Nos 3 and 4 Wings; top rt are the 'Old' and 'New' Workshops; Nos 1 and 2 Wings are off picture to right; while the grass airfield is further off picture to top right.   *MOD (Air)*

37
EVT — the educational programme for preparing RAF personnel for 'Civvy Street' on demobilisation.

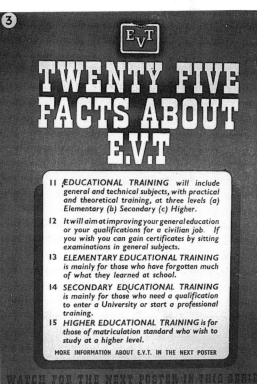

③

TWENTY FIVE FACTS ABOUT E.V.T

11 *EDUCATIONAL TRAINING will include general and technical subjects, with practical and theoretical training, at three levels (a) Elementary (b) Secondary (c) Higher.*

12 *It will aim at improving your general education or your qualifications for a civilian job. If you wish you can gain certificates by sitting examinations in general subjects.*

13 *ELEMENTARY EDUCATIONAL TRAINING is mainly for those who have forgotten much of what they learned at school.*

14 *SECONDARY EDUCATIONAL TRAINING is mainly for those who need a qualification to enter a University or start a professional training.*

15 *HIGHER EDUCATIONAL TRAINING is for those of matriculation standard who wish to study at a higher level.*

MORE INFORMATION ABOUT E.V.T. IN THE NEXT POSTER

WATCH FOR THE NEXT POSTER IN THIS SERIES

or civilian recruits with established technical qualifications. At its numerical peak the RAF had some 140,000 men and women under some form of training in air and (mainly) ground trades. Yet, curiously, the RAF had never established any particular 'trade' of instructor, apart from such obvious branches as Education Officers and Physical Training Instructors (PTIs) and the like. Technical instructors were (indeed, still are) in the main normal technical tradesmen of NCO, SNCO or commissioned rank, given a few weeks insight into the technique and psychological aspects of 'teaching', then 'detached' from more normal trade duties to a Technical Training School for a stipulated 'tour' of duty as an instructor. The only 'permanent' instructors were (and are) civilians, often ex-regular Servicemen, or possessing specialist civilian qualifications in the trade they teach.

Bomber Command

On 3 September 1939 RAF Bomber Command comprised five Groups (Nos 1 to 5) of operational squadrons, plus No 6 Group tasked with a training role. Command HQ was then situated at Richings Park, Langley in Buckinghamshire, though this moved to Naphill, near High Wycombe in March 1940. Its total of 53 squadrons included 20 'non-operational' units designated as Reserve or Group Pool Squadrons; while the aircraft flown by all units were divided between five main types of bomber:

Bristol Blenheim I and IV:	231 (1,809*)
Fairey Battle:	240 (1,014)
Armstrong Whitworth Whitley:	169 (196)
Vickers Wellington:	160 (175)
Handley Page Hampden:	140 (212)

Bracketed figures here show the RAF's total 'stock' by type on that date; the 'stock' figure for Blenheims* including 111 Blenheim IF modified fighter conversions with Fighter Command. Strictly, the whole of No 1 Group — 10 Battle squadrons — had in fact left Britain on 2 September and flown en masse to France, there to form the bomber element of the

Advanced Air Striking Force (AASF), and were to all intents and purposes no longer part of the UK-based Command. Thus, the Command in Britain had less than 400 operational bombers with which to pursue any form of bombing offensive against Germany.

Apart from its numerical weakness, Bomber Command's potential as an offensive force was severely restricted in a variety of ways at that time. Its crews, though extremely well-versed in actual flying standards, were in the main poorly experienced in long-range flights, particularly by night with its concomitant problems of precise navigation. Even by day relatively few crews had ever flown with a full bombload aboard their aircraft. Actual equipment for their prime role was barely adequate. Fuel tanks and systems were unprotected against bullet or shell damage, heating for high altitude flights was lacking for men or mechanical items, defensive armament against

38

Armstrong Whitworth Whitley — one of Bomber Command's early stalwarts, 1939-41; this example being from 78 Sqn.

39

Bumphleteers . . . Whitley crews of 77 Sqn loading propaganda leaflets for delivery to Germany from Topcliffe, early 1941. Note Cpl Wop/AG still wears the prewar brass 'flying bullet' badge of the air gunner on his tunic sleeve.

enemy fighter onslaught relied still upon hand-operated machine guns of rifle calibre, while the contemporary conception of self-defending bombers, needing no fighter escort, was of 1918 vintage outlook for day operations. Even the targets permitted to be bombed were confined strictly to 'naval objectives' — actual bombing of Germany itself with its consequent possibility of killing German civilians was vetoed. Accordingly, the earliest ventures over the German homeland were simply to 'bombard' the enemy with millions of propaganda leaflets only; while bombing sorties attempting to seek out the German navy by day incurred high casualties from intercepting Luftwaffe fighters.

The experience of the 1939-40 crews led to many minor technical modifications to aircraft for greater efficiency, but the prime difficulty in navigating to and locating and bombing specific targets accurately remained unresolved. A measure of the inaccuracy of the early operations was the statement by ACM Sir Richard Peirse on becoming AOC-in-C, Bomber Command in October 1940, that only one in five bombers despatched even found their designated targets, and even this 20% made

bombing errors from five to 100 miles from that target. During that first 12 months of the bombers' war some 12,000 individual sorties had been flown, dropping a gross total of 6,766 tons of bombs. In that same period 1,381 air crew men were killed, 419 became prisoners of war, 269 were wounded — all on operations. Nearly 600 others had died or been injured in 'non-operational' spheres — mainly during training. Overall, a total of almost 2,700 bomber men were effectively 'removed' from firstline employment — equivalent to more than the Command's entire operational crew strength in September 1939.

The year 1941 brought little effective change in actual bombing results, though new squadrons were steadily added to Command strength, and fresh bomber aircraft types were slowly introduced, the first true 'heavy' to reach a squadron being the Short Stirling, soon followed by the Handley Page Halifax, Avro Manchester, Boeing B-17 Fortress, and by no means least the De Havilland Mosquito. Of these only the Mosquito could be considered successful from the outset; the others suffering lengthy 'teething' troubles technically and tactically on initial operations. In December, however, the first redesigned Manchesters — now named Lancaster — entered first-line service; an aircraft destined to become Bomber Command's prime weapon thereafter. It was a year which also saw the introduction of the first radar and radio aids to navigation and bombing, such as 'GEE' and 'Trinity' — the latter a crude form of the later 'Oboe' device

40
Wimpy — Vickers Wellington T2468 of 9 Sqn at Honington, August 1940; another bomber stalwart which ultimately served throughout the war, and was produced in greater quantity than *any* other RAF bomber before or since. *R. D. Cooling*

for accurate navigation and bombing. For the bomber crews it was a year of intensified efforts, with a total of 27,101 sorties by night and 3,507 by day; but inevitably casualties mounted too. A total of 914 aircraft were lost on operations, with a further 300 at least being wrecked on return from sorties; in human terms, some 4,000 crew men killed, 'missing', prisoner, or seriously wounded. Significantly, at least 421 RAF bombers lost at night were shot down by German night fighters (compared to only 42 in 1940); a pointer to the escalating efficiency of Germany's air defences opposing the RAF bomber crews.

If 1941 saw the real start of the deadly night battles over the Reich, it was also a year in which the whole future of Bomber Command

was at risk. The alarming successes of Germany's U-boat depredations among the merchant shipping of Britain's supply lifelines across the North Atlantic gave ample reason for the Admiralty, and Coastal Command, to demand the detachment of sections of Bomber Command for increasing the aerial defences of those vital convoys. Added to the Command's seeming inability to cause any significant damage to Germany by bombing, there seemed to be good reasons for segmenting Bomber Command for more important roles. It was this delicate situation that AVM Sir Arthur Harris inherited on taking up his appointment as AOC-in-C, Bomber Command on 23 February 1942. On that date his Command could count

41
Bristol Blenheims formed the largest number of a single type of bomber available at the outbreak of war. This Mk IV, R3600, belonged to 82 Sqn, Wyton, and is being refuelled before the armourers load it with 250lb GP/HE bombs and SBCs (Small Bomb Containers) of 4lb Incendiaries. *IWM*

only 58 squadrons, seven of which were non-operational temporarily; little more than 600 aircraft actually available for operations, and less than 100 of these four-engined 'heavy' bombers. Harris decided to mount three ultra-heavy raids against key German cities — Cologne, Essen and Bremen — using 1,000 bombers in each attack, the first of these, against Cologne, taking place on the night of 30/31 May 1942. It proved successful, and the massive propaganda effect of Bomber Command being (apparently) able to despatch such an unprecedented number of aircraft succeeded in nullifying any further attempts to 'dissect' the Command for other uses.

Having 'secured' his Command by what amounted to a confidence trick, Harris then concentrated on building the strength of his squadrons, and providing better means and methods for ensuring optimum damage to Germany. One such innovation was the creation of the Path Finder Force (PFF) in August 1942, which was intended as the future specialist force to spearhead main bomber raids by accurate location, marking, and bombing designated targets. By 3 September 1942 — virtually the 'halfway mark' of the entire war — the cost of Bomber Command's unceasing offensive during the first three years presented a grim tabulation of statistics. During the course of flying a total of 86,800 sorties, Bomber Command air crew casualties had been 11,366 killed, 2,814 prisoners of war and a further 1,655 wounded or seriously injured; while another 2,539 had been killed and 1,538 injured in 'non-operational' activities, primarily during some stage of training. In all, almost exactly 20,000 air crew men had been killed or crippled, or were 'guests' of the Third Reich.

By that stage of the war all air crew men knew that, on joining an operational squadron, they would be expected to fly at least 30 completed sorties as a first tour of duty,* after which they would normally expect to be 'rested' for six months or longer before becoming liable for recall for a second tour. Those who survived two tours of operations would then become permanently non-operational unless they *voluntarily* requested to stay on operations. Of approximately 125,000 air crew men who served with Bomber Command at some stage of the war, less than 60% survived the war; yet of those who completed a full first tour of operations, almost 7,000 *volunteered* for a second tour, and many hundreds continued to a third.

By March 1943 Bomber Command strength had risen to 65 squadrons, of which 37 were operating four-engined 'heavies', and in that month Harris launched his so-termed 'Battle of the Ruhr'. On 16/17 May Wg Cdr Guy Gibson led No 617 Squadron to destroy the Möhne, Eder and Sorpe dams; on the night of 24/25 July Operation 'Gomorrah' — the devastation

42

Flying Suitcase — the nickname for the Handley Page Hampden, a type which comprised some 25% of Bomber Command's operational strength in September 1939. Here AE288 of 408 Sqn RCAF is pictured at Syerston on 30 September 1941.
Public Archives of Canada

*In the PFF a first tour comprised a minimum of 45 sorties.

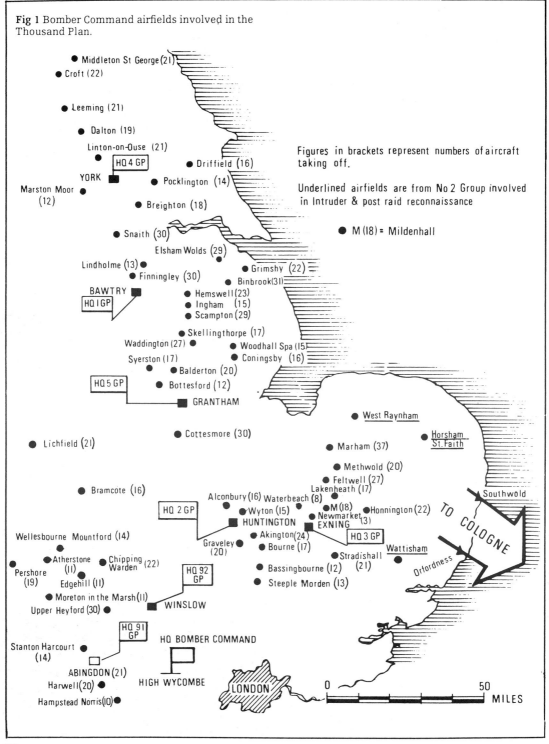

Fig 1 Bomber Command airfields involved in the Thousand Plan.

Figures in brackets represent numbers of aircraft taking off.

Underlined airfields are from No 2 Group involved in Intruder & post raid reconnaissance

M (18) = Mildenhall

Middleton St George (21)
Croft (22)
Leeming (21)
Dalton (19)
Linton-on-Ouse (21)
HQ 4 GP
YORK
Driffield (16)
Marston Moor (12)
Pocklington (14)
Breighton (18)
Snaith (30)
Elsham Wolds (29)
Lindholme (13)
Finningley (30)
Grimsby (22)
Binbrook (31)
BAWTRY
HQ I GP
Hemswell (23)
Ingham (15)
Scampton (29)
Skellingthorpe (17)
Waddington (27)
Woodhall Spa (15)
Syerston (17)
Coningsby (16)
Balderton (20)
HQ 5 GP
Bottesford (12)
GRANTHAM
West Raynham
Cottesmore (30)
Lichfield (21)
Horsham St. Faith
Marham (37)
Methwold (20)
Feltwell (27)
Bramcote (16)
Lakenheath (17)
Alconbury (16)
Waterbeach (8)
Southwold
HQ 2 GP
Wyton (15)
M (18)
Honnington (22)
Newmarket (3)
HUNTINGTON
EXNING
Wellesbourne Mountford (14)
Akington (24)
HQ 3 GP
Graveley (20)
Bourne (17)
Atherstone (11)
Chipping Warden (22)
Stradishall (21)
Wattisham
Pershore (19)
Bassingbourne (12)
Edgehill (11)
HQ 92 GP
Steeple Morden (13)
Orfordness
Moreton in the Marsh (11)
Upper Heyford (30)
WINSLOW
TO COLOGNE
HQ 91 GP
HQ BOMBER COMMAND
Stanton Harcourt (14)
ABINGDON (21)
HIGH WYCOMBE
Harwell (20)
Hampstead Norris (10)
LONDON

0   50
MILES

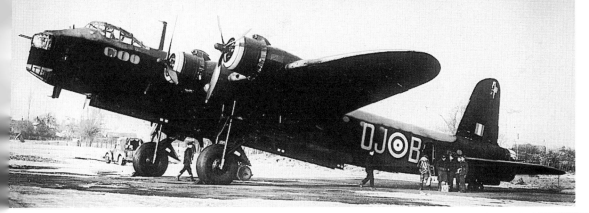

43
The mighty Stirling, which first entered RAF service in mid-1940 with 7 Sqn. This example, W7455, OJ-B, was with 149 Sqn at Mildenhall in January 1942.

of the city of Hamburg — was begun; while on 17/18 August nearly 600 bombers blasted the German rocket missile research establishment at Peenemunde, with Grp Capt John Searby acting as 'Master of Ceremonies' — a role used thereafter retitled Master Bomber in major raids. 1943 also saw the operational introduction of such new radar and radio sets as 'Airborne Cigar' and 'G-H', the giant 12,000lb HC/HE bomb, first dropped 'in anger' by 617 Squadron on 15/16 September on the Dortmund-Ems Canal, and a variety of new pyrotechnic marking and target-illuminating stores. Commencing on 18/19 November Harris inaugurated the 'Battle of Berlin' which continued until March 1944 — and cost 492 aircraft 'missing' and a further 954 'damaged' (including almost 100 completely wrecked on return from operations). From April 1943 to March 1944 — the most intensive period of Bomber Command operations of the war — a total of 2,703 bombers 'failed to return', representing the loss of almost exactly 19,000 air crew members; the rough equivalent of 130 complete Lancaster squadrons. The chief cause of casualties had been the Luftwaffe's night fighter force which, from November 1943 to March 1944 alone, had claimed slightly more than 1,000 victims among the bomber streams.

From April 1944 Bomber Command came under the general direction of the supreme Allied commander, General Eisenhower, and was ordered to switch its main efforts to disruption of all forms of transportation in France leading to the proposed Allied invasion zones in Normandy, and in the seven weeks prior to

44
Second four-engined 'heavy' to enter RAF operational use in WW2 was the Halifax, in March 1941. TL-P here was one of 35 Sqn's machines in 1942.

45
'Time-honour'd Lancaster' . . . Bomber Command's greatest night bomber of 1941-45. This dusk scene was at Scampton, with Lancs of 83 Sqn being readied for the night's operations.

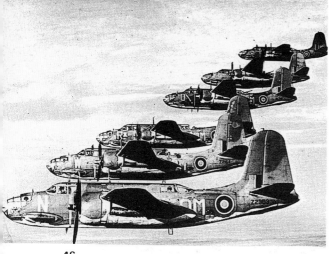

46
One of many American-designed bombers used extensively by the RAF was the Douglas Boston; this echelon belonging to 107 Sqn.

6 June — D-Day — the bombers dropped more than 42,000 tons of bombs and reduced the French transportation systems to a shambles. This 'aid' to the invasion forces culminated on the eve of D-Day when among other assaults 1,136 heavy bombers dropped 5,267 tons of bombs among 10 major enemy coastal batteries adjacent to the Normandy beaches and nullified their use. Once firmly ashore the invading forces continued to receive tactical help from Harris's crews who continued blast-

47
100-up. Crew of Lancaster R5868, PO-S, of 467 Sqn RAAF after 'Sugar's' purported 100th operational sortie in May 1944; its skipper on this occasion being Fg Off T. N. Scholefield (far left). R5868 now resides in the RAF Museum, Hendon, fully refurbished. *Central Press*

ing all German supply routes and installations, but a large proportion of Bomber Command now returned to continue its strategic attacks on German oil resources in co-operation with the USAAF's Eighth Air Force. By the autumn of 1944 Allied air supremacy over Europe had reached a point where heavy bombing raids could be made by day and by night, thereby increasing the sheer weight of destruction imposed upon Germany's dwindling resources. The final operations flown by Bomber Command came on the night of 2/3 May 1945 by a total of nearly 350 Mosquitos.

By then the Command had expanded to a total of nearly 100 firstline units, equipped with a gross total of 2,254 aircraft. Of these, Lancasters were being flown by no less than 57 squadrons, and 17 others had Halifaxes. The overall statistics of Bomber Command's total war effort showed that its crews had flown a total of 364,514 individual sorties, and dropped at least 955,044 tons of explosive 'stores'. Aircraft losses in action amounted to 8,325, apart from at least 16,000 others damaged in varying degrees. The cost in air crew lives was grievous — 47,268 men killed and 4,200 others wounded on actual operations, with 8,305 other crew men killed on 'non-operational' duties. Collectively this toll represented some 70% of total RAF personnel killed throughout the war in every facet of the struggle. The term 'RAF' here is perhaps misleading, inasmuch as no small proportion of casualties had been suffered by the many non-English members of the Command.

The majority of such men came from the various Commonwealth countries, and of those who gave their lives, the RAAF lost 3,412, the RCAF lost 8,209, the RNZAF 1,433, while 48 others came from other non-British origins.

AOC-in-Cs, Bomber Command, 1939-45

12 September 1937:	ACM Sir Edgar Ludlow-Hewitt KCB, CMG, DSO, MC
3 April 1940:	AM Sir Charles Portal KCB, DSO, MC
5 October 1940:	AM Sir Richard Peirse KCB, DSO, AFC
9 January 1942:	AVM J. E. A. Baldwin (Acting only)
23 February 1942:	ACM Sir Arthur Harris GCB, OBE, AFC
15 September 1945:	AM Sir Norman Bottomley KCB, CIE, DSO, AFC

No 8 (Path Finder) Group

While all other Bomber Command Groups during the war were continuations of existing peacetime organisations, albeit greatly and steadily expanded territorially and in strength, No 8 Group existed only during the war, being created to meet a vital operational need. Bearing in mind the initial operational difficulties of bomber crews being (mainly) unable to guarantee accurate navigation to and location of any specified target by night during the years 1939-41; the basic idea of a special / target-finders' force to spearhead main bomber streams soon began to gain credence. One of the initial 'champions' for such a force was Grp Capt (later, AVM) Sydney Bufton DSO, DFC, a bomber veteran who by late 1941 was serving at the Air Ministry as Deputy Director of Bomber Operations. His proposal was for a new formation, comprising six squadrons, based 'in close proximity to each other', manned by normal crews leavened by about 40 selected highly experienced crews from those available. With support for this concept, Bufton presented the suggestion to Arthur Harris, AOC-in-C, Bomber Command early in 1943, only to meet Harris's objections to any form of *corps d'elite* within his command. Harris, however, favoured the proposition of 'target-finders' or 'Raid Leaders' as he personally termed them — and proposed instead that one

49
Christmas Trees — the German nickname for the PFF's target indicator or pyrotechnic flares. These Lancasters were from 156 Sqn, over Hanau on the night of 18/19 March 1945.

48
Path Finder — Sqn Ldr Jack Partridge DSO, DFC of 83 Sqn, PFF, wearing the qualified PFF man's eagle brooch below his medal ribbons.
Sqn Ldr J. Partridge, DSO, DFC

squadron within each group should be selected for such duties. In the event Harris was over-ruled by higher authority, with the result that on 15 August 1942, the Path Finder Force (PFF) was brought into being.

With its headquarters at RAF Wyton, and commanded by Grp Capt D. C. T. Bennett, the PFF's 'founder' members were Nos 7 Squadron (Stirlings), 35 Squadron (Halifaxes), 83 Squadron (Lancasters) and 156 Squadron (Wellingtons). A fifth unit, No 109 Squadron (Mosquitos), was temporarily 'detached' to the PFF and tasked principally with development and operational testing of the new Oboe radar equipment. In this initial stage the PFF came under the administrative aegis of No 3 Group, but on 8 January 1943 the PFF was elevated in status to become No 8 Group, and its commander, Bennett, was promoted to Air Commodore, and later Air Vice-Marshal. With its mixture of differing types of bomber and few

35

fresh technical aids to accurate navigation or bombing, the first operations by the PFF gave little indication of any great improvement in ultimate success; though many of the force's crews were soon being joined by volunteer crews with reasonable experience in the business of bombing operations. Once established, the PFF's prime requisites for its future members were that they would be prepared to undertake first tour of at least 45 sorties — 50% more sorties than the usual tour required — and that each man should be a volunteer for PFF duties.

As the first few months passed the PFF slowly 'got into its stride' on the path to perfection. The Mosquitos of 109 Squadron, led by H. E. 'Hal' Bufton (brother of Syd) flew the first operational trials of Oboe on 20 December 1942, and in January 1943 two other new inventions were tested operationally — target indicating (TI) marker bombs on Berlin on 16/17 January, and H2S against Hamburg on 30 January. In June 1943 Bennett moved the PFF HQ from Wyton to nearby Castle Hill House, Huntingdon; while in April two more units came under his command — 405 Squadron RCAF at Gransden Lodge, and 97 Squadron (Lancasters) at Bourn. Early in June two more Mosquito squadrons joined with No 109 in developing and operating Oboe, these being Nos 105 and 139 Squadrons, based at Marham; while a fourth Mosquito squadron, No 627, was added to the PFF in November 1943, and a fifth, No 692 Squadron, joined them on 1 January 1944. A further boost to PFF's heavy bomber strength came in March 1944 with the arrival of No 635 Squadron (Lancasters), then in April No 582 Squadron. However, in the latter month Don Bennett lost three units, Nos 83, 97 and 627 Squadrons, all three being 'detached' by higher authority to No 5 Group in order to assist that group's individual ideas on pathfinding techniques.

Despite the loss of those three pioneering units, the PFF continued to expand, particularly in regard to its Mosquito units which by then had been formed into what Bennett himself termed the Light Night Striking Force (LNSF). In August 1944 No 608 Squadron joined the LNSF, while by January 1945 four more Mosquito units had arrived, Nos 128, 142, 162 and 163 Squadrons. Most of these

Mosquitos were capable of carrying one 4,000lb HC 'Cookie' bomb to targets as far afield as Berlin, thereby adding considerable weight to the PFF's destructive attacks on Germany. By April 1945 the PFF had reached its wartime peak of strength, with totals of six Lancaster and 10 Mosquito squadrons, as under:

Squadron	Base	Aircraft on charge
7	Oakington	21 Lancasters
35	Graveley	25 Lancasters
156	Upwood	21 Lancasters
405 RCAF	Gransden Lodge	22 Lancasters
582	Little Staughton	22 Lancasters
635	Downham Market	20 Lancasters
105	Bourn	31 Mosquitos
109	Little Staughton	31 Mosquitos
128	Wyton	24 Mosquitos
139	Upwood	19 Mosquitos
142	Gransden Lodge	20 Mosquitos
162	Bourn	20 Mosquitos
163	Wyton	18 Mosquitos
571	Oakington	21 Mosquitos
608	Downham Market	26 Mosquitos
692	Graveley	28 Mosquitos

In addition, officially, Nos 83, 97 and 627 Squadrons, though still operating with No 5 Group, remained on the PFF's paper 'strength'.

With the surrender of Germany in May 1945 the PFF's brief war record revealed the extent of its prowess — and sacrifice. Its crews had flown a gross total of 50,490 individual sorties (including the LNSF) against some 3,440 targets. The cost in crews had been at least 3,727 men killed on operations alone — the rough equivalent of 20 Lancaster squadrons — while many hundreds of others had been injured to some degree. Such a figure represented approximately one-sixth of Bomber Command's total fatal casualties for its entire war period. Of the 32 airmen awarded a Victoria Cross during 1939-45, Bomber Command air crew men had received 21 — and three of these went to PFF pilots, all posthumously. On 12 May 1945 AVM Bennett was succeeded as AOC by AVM J. R. Whitley, and on 15 December 1945 No 8 (PFF) Group was quietly disbanded.

Fighter Command

As with Bomber, Coastal and Training Commands, RAF Fighter Command came into being as an entity with effect from 14 July 1936, its HQ being at Bentley Priory, near Stanmore, and its first commander being Air Marshal (later, ACM, Lord) Hugh Dowding. Dowding's initial command included four main internal formations; Nos 11 and 12 Groups of fighter squadrons, No 22 Army Co-operation Group (for administrative purposes only), and the civilian-manned Observer Corps. In actual fighter strength, the Command then possessed 18 squadrons, all equipped with biplane aircraft. By 1 September 1939 the Command had expanded rapidly. On that date its strength stood at 37 squadrons, 14 of these recently mobilised Auxiliary Air Force (AAF) units. Overall, 17 squadrons were flying Hurricanes, 12 had Spitfires, and six were equipped with stop-gap, modified Blenheim IF 'fighters'. Between them the squadrons had the following totals of aircraft:

Hurricane:	347 (400)
Spitfire:	187 (270)
Blenheim IF:	111 (111)
Gladiator:	76 (218)
Gauntlet:	26 (100)

The bracketed figures were totals on overall RAF charge then; thus, of a complete 'stock' of 1,099 fighters, the Command's firstline squadrons had 747 machines.

Despite the tragic losses by Fighter Command in men and machines detached from the UK defence to participate in operations over France and such 'sideshows' as the ill-starred Norwegian interlude — campaigns which had cost the RAF the losses of 432 Hurricanes and Spitfires between 10 May and 18 June 1940 over France and Dunkirk alone — by 1 July 1940 Fighter Command showed a firstline strength of 51 operational squadrons, with six more working up to that status. These were distributed between Nos 11, 12 and 13 Groups defending the key southern and south-east coasts of England, and were manned by a gross total of 1,103 fighter pilots — 11 Group having 553, 12 Group 228, and 13 Group 322, or little more than 1,000 young men to oppose the expected Luftwaffe prelude onslaught to Hitler's planned invasion of Britain in that fateful summer. In the so-termed Battle of Britain which followed — the official dates for which were from 10 July to 31 October 1940 inclusive — Fighter Command lost 481 men killed or listed as 'Missing', while a further 422 were seriously injured or wounded. Total aircraft losses, both destroyed or written off charge due to unrepairable damage, amounted to 1,140. In 'balance' Fighter Command had destroyed at least 1,733 German aircraft, and damaged a further 643 in varying degrees; but its prime objective — the prevention of a German invasion — had been achieved conclusively.

By November 1940 the Luftwaffe's assault on Britain had begun to switch emphasis from day to night operations — the beginning of the 1940-41 winter blitz. Fighter Command's meagre night fighter element in that month totalled 12 squadrons, six of which were operating Blenheim Is and Beaufighters fitted with the early forms of Airborne Interception AI radar sets . By May 1941 this overall total had increased to 16 squadrons, half of which still relied upon unsuitable — for nightfighting interception roles — Hurricanes and Defiants. Nevertheless, the remaining eight squadrons, using their radar, and controlled from — by July 1941 — 17 GCI (Ground Control Installations), achieved mounting successes against the German bombers; claiming 22 victims in March 1941, and no less than 96 in May.

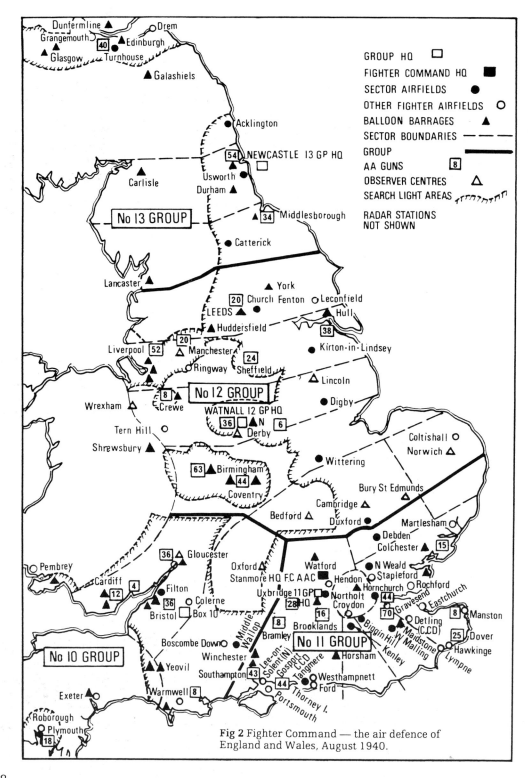

GROUP HQ □
FIGHTER COMMAND HQ ■
SECTOR AIRFIELDS ●
OTHER FIGHTER AIRFIELDS ○
BALLOON BARRAGES ▲
SECTOR BOUNDARIES ----
GROUP ▬
AA GUNS 8
OBSERVER CENTRES △
SEARCH LIGHT AREAS
RADAR STATIONS
NOT SHOWN

Dunfermline ▲
Drem ○
Grangemouth ▲
40 Edinburgh ●
Glasgow ▲ Turnhouse ▲
Galashiels ▲

Acklington ●

54 NEWCASTLE 13 GP HQ □
Usworth ●
Carlisle ▲
Durham ▲

No 13 GROUP

34 Middlesborough ▲

Catterick ●

Lancaster ▲

York ▲
20 Church Fenton ● Leconfield ○
LEEDS ▲ Hull ▲
Huddersfield ▲ 38
Liverpool 52 20 Manchester △
Ringway ▲ Sheffield 24 Lincoln △
Kirton-in-Lindsey ●
Wrexham △ Crewe ▲ No 12 GROUP Digby ●
8 WATNALL 12 GP HQ □
Tern Hill ○ 36 □ N 6
Shrewsbury ▲ △ Derby Coltishall ○
Norwich △
63 ▲ Birmingham Wittering ●
44 ▲
Coventry Bury St Edmunds △
Cambridge △
Bedford △ Duxford ●
Martlesham ○
Debden ●
Colchester ▲ 15
36 △ Gloucester
Pembrey ○ Oxford △ Watford ▲ N Weald ●
Stanmore HQ F.C AAC Stapleford ●
Cardiff ▲ 4 Hendon ■ Hornchurch ● Rochford ○
12 Filton ▲ Uxbridge 11 GP 44 Gravesend ▲ Eastchurch
Bristol □ 36 Colerne □ 28 HQ Northolt ● 70 Detling 8
Box 10 16 Croydon ● (CCD) 25 Manston
8 Brooklands ● Biggin Hill ● Dover ○
Boscombe Down ● No 11 GROUP W Malling Hawkinge
Bramley ▲ Kenley Lympne
No 10 GROUP Winchester Lee-on-Solent (N) ○ Horsham ▲
Yeovil ▲ Middle Wallop Gosport CCD
Southampton 43 Tangmere ● Westhampnett
Exeter ○ 44 Ford ●
Warmwell 8 Thorney I. ○
Roborough Portsmouth
Plymouth ○
18

Fig 2 Fighter Command — the air defence of
England and Wales, August 1940.

During the same period the Command began night 'intrusion' operations on a small scale — despatching individual 'free-lance' fighters to attack German bomber airfields in France.

In December 1940 several small fighter sorties inaugurated what amounted to a future major role for the Command — daylight *offensive* sweeps over enemy-occupied territories. Though still acknowledged as primarily a metropolitan aerial *defence* organisation, Fighter Command henceforth was to become the 'rapier' of the RAF's struggle against the Luftwaffe. This offensive tone for fighter opera-

50 & 51
The immortal Hurricane, backbone of RAF fighter offensive. Above (50) Hurricane I, N2358 of No 1 Sqn, 1940; and below (51) a Mk IIC, BE500 of 87 Sqn in all-black nightfighter livery, with the unit Co, Sqn Ldr Dennis Smallwood DFC in his 'office'.
C. E. Brown

tions was reflected throughout 1941 in various forms of day sorties, including 'Rhubarbs' and 'Circus'-style operations aimed primarily at drawing up German fighters into battles of plain attrition. The outcome of the 'Circus'

52
Fighter sweep — Spitfires setting out from Northolt, mid-1941. *IWM*

operations during 1941 was by no means as successful as either hoped or, indeed, claimed at that time. This can be part-illustrated by the results of such sorties during six weeks in June-July 1941. In 46 such operations the RAF lost 123 fighter pilots, declared 'Missing'. During the same six weeks RAF pilots involved claimed a total of 322 German aircraft destroyed — a figure grossly overestimated, and greater than the entire Luftwaffe fighter strength based in France at that period. Another, equally costly, form of offensive operation undertaken by the Command in 1941 was the 'Roadstead'; a combined fighter and light bomber operation aimed against enemy surface shipping along the English Channel and adjacent seaways. For these types of sorties Hurricanes and Whirlwind fighters were modified to carry 250lb or 500lb HE bombs in addition to their normal cannon armament. Again, the ratio of RAF losses against claimed successes was to prove distinctly 'unprofitable'.

In the context of organisation Fighter Command steadily expanded from five groups and 23 sectors in November 1940 to six operational groups and 29 sectors by the spring of 1941; while by April 1941 Command strength totalled 81 squadrons — 16 of these being designated as night fighter units. The average paper-establishment for pilots on a fighter squadron was at last 26, though actual

strength was seldom more than 22 pilots per unit. Though factory production of aircraft, and air crew training organisations, were by now able to guarantee a reasonably plentiful supply of machines and men for further expansion, the priority claims for both 'products' to bolster RAF strength in various overseas operational theatres diluted the supply of home-based Commands in 1941-42. Added 'muscle' for Fighter Command also arrived in

53
Knight in armour. Fighter pilot of No 1 Sqn RCAF, 1940 wearing flying helmet, goggles with sun-glare visor, oxygen and R/T mask. Note top tunic button unfastened — the unofficial mark of the fighter pilot then. *Public Archives of Canada*

54
Army Co-op. North American Mustangs of 2 Sqn RAF at Sawbridgeworth in July 1942, tasked with level tactical support for the Army.

the shape of fresh aircraft types and improved variants of the standard Hurricane and Spitfire stalwarts; the most significant of these being the AI-equipped Beaufighter and, especially, the Mosquito — the latter for both night and day operations by mid-1942. In 1942, too, Fighter Command was called upon for its greatest one-day operational effort to date when, on 19 August, it provided a constant aerial 'umbrella' protection for the Allied attack on Dieppe. From pre-dawn until mid-afternoon Fighter Command despatched

approximately 60% of the RAF's total of 2,955 individual sorties over Dieppe. At the end of the day RAF losses were acknowledged as 106 aircraft, while RAF claims for totals of 91 German aircraft destroyed and nearly 200 others damaged or probably destroyed bore little relation to the actual German losses of 48 destroyed and 24 damaged. What the RAF could not know, however, was that the German fighter strength in France by the end of the Dieppe battle had been reduced to just 70 serviceable fighters. Hypothetically speaking,

55
The 'Crikey', or Westland Whirlwind fighter-bomber; another low-level fighter used in small numbers.

56
'Tiffy' — Hawker Typhoon Ib, JP401 of 439 Sqn RCAF landing at a forward airfield in Germany during the final phase of the war.
Public Archives of Canada

had the pace of the Dieppe aerial fighting continued for one more day, the RAF would have achieved within 48 hours all that it had been attempting to do for the previous 18 months of 'Circus' and similar operations, ie render Luftwaffe opposition in France effectively *hors de combat*.

As the winter of 1942-43 closed in, the Luftwaffe resumed its assaults against principal British cities, albeit on a much reduced scale from the 1940-41 blitz, while a relatively new form of such raids was undertaken by bomb-carrying Focke-Wulf FW190 fighters which, sporadically, flew a series of low-level 'sneak' attacks against south-east England targets from October 1942 until June 1943. Fighter Command defenders by then included Spitfire XIIs and Hawker Typhoons, each type capable of matching an FW190 at

low altitudes, while the night fighter defences included 12 squadrons of AI-equipped Beaufighters, six more flying radar-equipped Mosquitos, with four more Mosquito units in the process of receiving their new 'Wooden Wonder' fighters; a night force totalling some 400 machines. The high proportional loss rates among the FW190 sneak raiders soon nullified this particular type of raid, but the night forays continued erratically through the winter of 1943-44 on a diminishing scale, again suffering relatively high losses to RAF night defenders.

Meanwhile, in 1943, the overall Allied Command was preparing slowly for the invasion of France — the so-termed 'Second Front' — and the first stage of reorganisation of the Allied air services began on 1 June 1943, when No 2 Group, Bomber Command's light and medium bomber force was transferred to the aegis of Fighter Command. It was the first of several stages, aimed at creating an air formation separate from existing Commands, for exclusive use alongside the Allied Expeditionary Force being formed for the invasion itself. On 13 November 1943 the Allied Expeditionary Air Force (AEAF) came into being, with ACM Sir Trafford Leigh-Mallory as its appointed commander. The new force comprised three main components. One, already existing, was the USAAF's 9th Air Force, while the others — officially 'formed' two days later — were the Second Tactical Air Force (2nd TAF) and the Air Defence of Great Britain (ADGB). Second TAF effectively 'robbed' Fighter Command of 32 fighter squadrons, leaving just 10 day and 11 night fighter squadrons for the ADGB. Thus, on 15 November 1943, RAF Fighter Command *per se* ceased to exist, to be replaced in function and purpose by the ADGB, commanded by AM Roderic Hill, the former commander of No 12 Group. From then until the actual invasion date of 6 June 1944 — D-Day — ADGB was tasked with the aerial defence of Britain, but also with aerial 'security' over the gathering mass of men and materials in southern England as the invasion forces steadily assembled in preparation.

On 13 June 1944, however, the ADGB was suddenly faced with a new menace to Britain,

as the first Fieseler 103 robot flying bombs — usually titled V1s — arrived in England; harbingers of a mounting robot bomb offensive which was to continue until early 1945, supplemented from September 1944 by the larger V2 rocket missile — a 12.7 tons missile packing 1,650lb of high explosive which rose to an altitude of some 50 miles, then plunged on to its target at speeds calculated at more than 2,000mph; a weapon patently impossible to intercept by conventional aircraft means. The ADGB's response to the V1 threat included the use of the new Hawker Tempest and, from July 1944, the RAF's first jet-engined fighter, the Gloster Meteor. During the whole of the V1 'campaign', from 13 June 1944 to 29 March 1945, RAF fighters shot or brought down a total of 1,846 of the cruciform flying bombs; roughly 46% of all V1s destroyed by British defences of all types. Unable to prevent the V2 intercontinental missile by normal interception, RAF fighters participated in the RAF's general attacks against known V1 and V2 launching sites in France, Belgium and Holland.

By October 1944 the temporary reorganisation of the RAF's elements of the AEAF was no longer considered necessary, so with the much-reinforced 2nd TAF now capable of furnishing all aerial tactical support to the armies in Europe, on 15 October 1944 the ADGB title was discontinued for Roderic Hill's formation and RAF Fighter Command was re-established for UK-based fighter defences, with Hill remaining as AOC-in-C. Victory in Europe — VE-Day — was officially declared on 8 May 1945, and Fighter Command's war was over. The cost in human life of that war had been totals of 3,690 air crew men killed, a further 1,215 seriously wounded or injured, and 601 becoming prisoners of war.

AOC-in-Cs, Fighter Command, 1939-45

14 July 1936:	AM Sir Hugh C. T. Dowding KCB, CMG
25 November 1940:	AM W. S. Douglas CB, MC, DFC
28 November 1942:	AM T. L. Leigh-Mallory CB, DSO
15 November 1943:	AM R. M. Hill CB, MC, AFC

Fighter Command retitled as Air Defence of Great Britain wef 15 November 1943; retitled Fighter Command wef 15 October 1944

14 May 1945:	AM Sir James M. Robb KBE, CB, DSO, DFC, AFC

57
Fg Off Edgar Kain DFC of 73 Sqn RAF — the first five-victory fighter 'ace' of the RAF in WW2. A New Zealander, he was killed in a flying accident on 7 June 1940 in France.

RAF fighter pilots credited with at least 20 victories

The term 'ace' has never been officially defined or recognised by any British air Service. Nevertheless, certain fighter pilots serving under RAF operational control during 1939-45 were often credited with specific numbers of enemy aircraft 'destroyed' in award citations *et al*. The 'victory' totals listed below are *minimums*, officially 'confirmed', but reference to contemporary enemy records often indicate that — as was the case with fighter pilots in *all* air services — such claims were often exaggerated. Such 'over-claims' were made honestly, in good faith, in the heat of the lightning-like cut and thrust aerial combat, but should not always be regarded as finite tallies of enemy aircraft *actually* destroyed. It should be noted that, unlike the practice in the USAAF, enemy aircraft destroyed on the ground were *not* included in an RAF fighter pilot's 'score'; thus all 'victories' listed here were claimed from aerial combat only.

Name	Credited score
Pattle, Marmaduke Thomas St John:	41+
Johnson, James Edgar	38
Malan, Adolph Gysbert	35
Clostermann, Pierre	33
Finucane, Brendan	32
Beurling, George Frederick	31
Braham, John Robert Daniel	29
Tuck, Roland Robert Stanford	29*
Duke, Neville Frederick	28
Caldwell, Clive Robertson	28
Carey, Frank Reginald	28+†
Lacey, James Harry	28
Gray, Colin Falkland	28
Lock, Eric Stanley	26
Wade, Lance	25
Drake, Billy	25
Vale, William	24‡
Allard, Geoffrey	24
Le Roux, Johannes Jacobus	24
Bader, Douglas Robert Steuart	23
Boyd, Robert Finlay	23
Kingaby, Donald Ernest	23
Stephen, Harbourne Mackay	23
Crossley, Michael Nicholson	22
Dalton-Morgan, Thomas Frederick	22
Deere, Alan Christopher	22
Hugo, Petrus Hendrik	22
Mackie, Evan Dall	22
Stephens, Maurice Michael	22
Woodward, Vernon Crompton	22
Crawford-Compton, William Vernon	22
Hesselyn, Ray Brown	22
Hallowes, Herbert James Lampriere	22
Burbridge, Bransome Arthur	21
Demozay, Jean	21
Gilroy, George Kemp	21
Hewett, Edward William Foott	21
McKellar, Archie Ashmore	21
McLeod, Henry Wallace	21
Rankin, James	21
Harries, Raymond Hiley	20
Cunningham, John	20
David, William Dennis	20
Lovell, Anthony Desmond Joseph	20
McMullen, Desmond Annesley Peter	20

*30 postwar
†*Evidence suggests this is an understatement tally*
‡*Some sources say 28*

58
Sqn Ldr M. T. St J. Pattle DFC — the highest-scoring RAF pilot of 1939-45 who was killed in action over Athens on 20 April 1941.

59
'Sailor' — Gp Capt A. G. Malan DSO, DFC, a South African who was acknowledged as possibly the greatest RAF fighter leader of the war. *IWM*

60
Wg Cdr Brendan Finucane DSO, DFC, a 32-victory 'ace' who died on 15 July 1942. Of Irish origin, he is seen here, far right, at Kirton-in-Lindsey while serving as a flight commander with 452 Sqn RAAF.

61
Belgian pilots with 609 Sqn, and the unit mascot 'Wing Commander William' perched upon Charles de Moulin's shoulders.

62
Spitfire pilots, on return from a daylight sortie on 29 April 1942 are greeted by HM King George VI. *Associated Press*

63
Grp Capt J. E. Johnson DSO, DFC, the highest-scoring RAF fighter pilot in the European war theatre. *IWM*

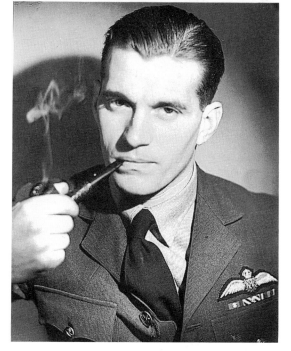

Of these 45 pilots, 17 were not British-born, coming from New Zealand (5), South Africa (4), Canada (3), France (2), and Eire, Australia and the USA (one from each). Eleven of these 45 pilots were killed before the end of the war. If one accepts the oft-quoted definition of an 'ace' as being one who is credited with at least five enemy aircraft destroyed in aerial combat; the RAF could claim at least 1,017 'aces' during 1939-45, ie men whose claims were confirmed while operating under RAF control. Dozens of other 'non-British' fighter pilots who became 'aces' while serving with other Allied air forces later accrued their first two or three 'victories' while with the RAF.

Coastal Command

Officially created on 14 July 1936, Coastal Command on that date comprised a mere eight squadrons, equipped with six different types of aircraft. Headquarters of the Command then was at Lee-on-Solent, controlling (on paper) three groups (Nos 15, 16 and 17), two of which had yet to be inaugurated, plus administration and post-FTS training of the Fleet Air Arm, and a small detachment of the Command at Bermuda. In 1937 Command HQ was moved en bloc to a private house, Eastbury Park, at Northwood, near Watford, where it was to remain for the war years. On 24 July 1939 the Command received its mobilisation orders, in order to bring all units to the following state by 14 August 1939:

HQCC, Northwood

HQ 15 Group Plymouth	HQ 16 Group Gillingham	HQ 17 Group Gosport	HQ 18 Group Pitreavie
Mountbatten	Bircham Newton	Calshot	SS *Manela*
Pembroke Dock	Thorney Island	Thorney Island	Invergordon
Warmwell	Detling		Woodhaven
Carew Cheriton	Guernsey Airport		Montrose
Aldergrove			Leuchars

The various Group functions, though flexible, were defined as:

Anti-submarine patrols:	15 & 18
Anti-shipping:	16 & 18
CC operational training:	17
ASR & Meteorological Flights:	All Groups
Photo-reconnaissance Unit:	106

Actual aircraft strength of the Command on 3 September 1939 was:

Avro Anson:	301
Lockheed Hudson:	53
Vickers Vildebeest:	30
Short Sunderland:	27
Saro London:	17
Supermarine Stranraer:	9

In addition were a few individual communications aircraft, making a gross total of nearly 450 aircraft; though less than 300 could correctly be termed as 'operationally available' on that date. With regard to personnel serving under the aegis of Coastal Command total strength did not exceed 10,000, all ranks. Nevertheless, on 3 September 1939 the Command comprised four groups, one wing and eight other stations. By December 1941 this organisation had expanded to six groups, three wings, and 33 other stations; spread amongst which were 55,735 RAF and 6,223 WAAF of all ranks.

The prime functions of Coastal Command throughout the war remained constant; protection of merchant shipping, anti-submarine patrols, anti-shipping attacks, mine-laying and — from 1941 — overall responsibility for air-sea rescue organisation. Thus its crews alternated between defensive and offensive operations — a reflection of the Command's official motto 'Constant Endeavour'. The multi-variation in duties involved ever-changing equipment, including the operational use of some 50 different types of aircraft ranging from humble DH Tiger Moths to Very Long Range (VLR) versions of the American Consolidated B-24 Liberator, Catalina, and Boeing B-17 Fortress. The Command's quantitative 'muscle' also expanded rapidly as crews and aircraft became available, and by the close of the war no less than 85 squadrons had served either continuously or at least 'part-time' under Coastal Command operational control; apart from US Navy units, OTUs, etc etc.

In terms of operational 'action' — ie actual engagement with the enemy, be it ship, sub-

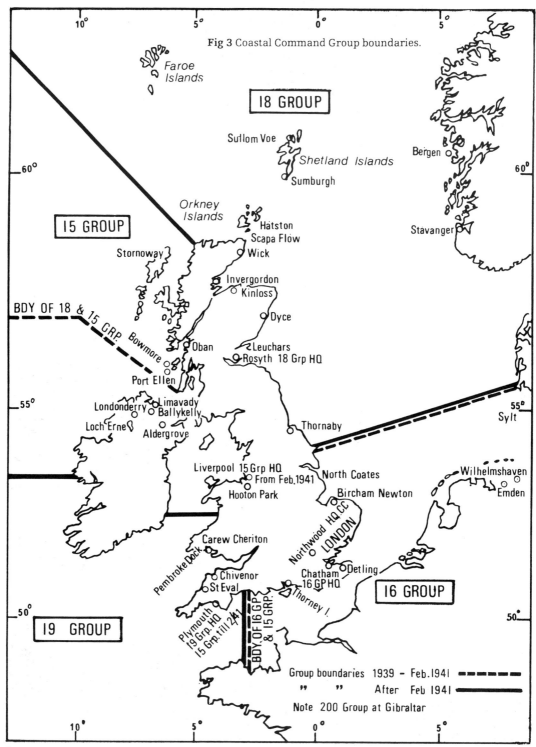

Fig 3 Coastal Command Group boundaries.

Faroe Islands

18 GROUP

Sullom Voe
Shetland Islands
Sumburgh

Bergen

Stavanger

Orkney Islands

15 GROUP

Hatston
Scapa Flow
Stornoway
Wick

Invergordon
Kinloss
Dyce

BDY OF 18 & 15 GRP. Bowmore
Oban
Leuchars
Port Ellen
Rosyth 18 Grp HQ

Limavady
Londonderry Ballykelly
Loch Erne
Aldergrove

Thornaby

Sylt

Liverpool 15 Grp HQ
From Feb.1941
Hooton Park

North Coates
Wilhelmshaven
Bircham Newton
Emden

Carew Cheriton

Northwood HQ C.C.
LONDON

Pembroke Dock

Chivenor
St Eval
Chatham
16 GP HQ
Detling

16 GROUP

Plymouth
19 Grp. HQ
15 Grp. till 2/41

BDY. OF 16 GP.
& 15 GRP.

Thorney I.

19 GROUP

Group boundaries 1939 – Feb.1941 ------
"   "   After Feb 1941 ——
Note 200 Group at Gibraltar

48

64
'Faithful Annie' — Avro Anson of 502 Sqn AAF on convoy escort patrol, 1940.

marine, aircraft, or anti-aircraft flak at land targets — Coastal Command crews spent the bulk of their flying hours in the drudgery of monotonous seas and ocean patrols 'watching water' — an ever-present deterrent to surfacing U-boats, a constant watch-dog shepherding the mercantile convoys. Such a role demanded stoic patience and unusual qualities of mental and physical endurance on the part of the crews; having to remain on the *qui vive* at all times and prepared to change from 'routine' to 'action stations' instantly when the need arose. As with all air crews to some degree, the Coastal men fought two enemies — the war machine of the Axis Powers, and raw nature. Of these, the latter was probably the greatest 'opponent' for the men of Coastal Command. The vast majority of operational flying hours was spent over the sea; an uncompromising, pitiless 'foe', offering no quarter or haven in the event of any crash or forced landing on its ever-shifting surface. It remains a sobering fact that more Coastal crews were 'lost' to this implacable 'enemy' than to any human adversary. The following summary of Coastal Command casualties for the entire war period gives some hint of the sacrifices made by the 'airmen of the seas':

Killed in action:	5,863
Killed in flying accidents:	2,261
Killed/died (other causes):	79
Missing, presumed dead:	5
Prisoners of War:	498
Wounded:	2,086

In addition, it should be remembered that Coastal ground crews suffered totals of 694 killed, 515 wounded, and 18 prisoners of war. Throughout the entire war the Command also lost a total of 2,053 aircraft — statistically speaking, the near-exact equivalent of one aircraft lost for *each* day of the war — while a further 1,441 aircraft were lost on operations 'outside' actual Command control.

The ultimate achievements of Coastal Command are not so easily summarised. The prime, single enemy sought was the

65
Lockheed Hudson III, T9465, literally a gift from its makers to the RAF, flew with 269 Sqn in 1941, based at Kaldadharnes, Iceland, on anti-submarine patrols. *British Official*

Unterseeboot (U-boat), whether at sea (mainly) or in harbour pen. A total of 1,162 submarines was commissioned into the German Navy of which an overall total of at least 727 was destroyed by Allied actions; while of approximately 40,000 men who served in U-boats crews, some 28,000 were killed in action, and a further 5,000 or so were taken prisoner. Of the 727 U-boats destroyed by Allied action:

288: sunk at sea by aircraft alone
  47: sunk at sea by combined air & RN action
  80: destroyed by strategic bombing raids

The remainder were lost in actions not involving air power. Coastal Command's contribution to these statistics was not small:

67
Short Sunderland ZM-W, 'Weary Willie' of 201 Sqn on ocean patrol, 28 October 1941.

66
German submarine U-570 surrendering to Hudson 'S' of 269 Sqn (pilot, Sqn Ldr J. H. Thompson) on 27 August 1941. The submarine was later used by the RN, retitled HMS *Graph*. *D. Lyall*

Claimed as sunk:	188
	(at least 192)
Claimed sunk & shared with RN:	24
	(at least 19)
Claimed damaged:	120
	(at least 131)

The figures bracketed are postwar researched evidence, as opposed to the unbracketed official claims.

Yet, despite these not inconsiderate war achievements, the ultimate value of Coastal crews' unceasing ward-and-watch role as shepherd-dogs for the merchant shipping convoys — the latter representing the British and Allied lifelines of resupply in every sense — cannot be measured in statistical tabulations. Only the U-boat crews can testify to the numerous occasions when the Damocles' sword of an aerial escort deterred submarines from attacking their unarmed prey — and almost 60% of those crews died at sea. Thus, it is impossible to compute the possible thousands of lives, hundreds of ships, or millions of tons of vital cargoes which were saved from a watery grave by the mere presence of a single Coastal Command aircraft and its faithful crew.

The general nature of Coastal Command's war can, in one sense at least, be divided roughly into two major 'phases'. For the first three years, 1939-42, operations were primarily concentrated upon defeating the predatory U-boats in the North Atlantic. For such operations, however, the Command was ill-equipped in the contexts of suitable aircraft and aids. Apart from purely Coastal designs, such as the Sunderland flying boat, Beaufort torpedo-bomber, and adapted Lockheed Hudsons etc, the Command was forced to 'borrow' aircraft and crews from Bomber Command, utilising modified Blenheims, Hampdens, Wellingtons, Whitleys and, briefly, even Lancasters, to bolster its armoury. By late 1942 the air-sea struggle was reaching its peak of activity, by which time the squadrons were re-equipping with four-engined VLR aircraft, such as the Liberator and Fortress, and thereby extending greatly their protective coverage of the seas, apart from using new radar and other technical aids for locating and destroying the common enemy. At that stage the Command inaugurated its first strike wing, comprising three squadrons of Beaufighters, based at North Coates. It was the first of several such wings to be formed subsequently, tasked solely with an offensive role, to attack enemy shiping, ports, installations and the like. As such the strike wings were 'solidifying' the past efforts of former Blenheim and Beaufort units in

68
Big Cat — Consolidated Catalina, AH550, of 210 Sqn, 1941.

69
Bristol Beaufighter TFX, NE355, EE-H of 404 Sqn RCAF at Davidstow Moor, Cornwall on 21 August 1944. The protrusion from the nose was a Fairchild camera mounting. *Public Archives of Canada*

stretching the 'long arm' of the Command. Their efforts, initially using Beaufighters, then the ubiquitous Mosquito, were maintained at ever-escalating pace until the very last days of the European war.

For the men and women who served in Coastal Command during the war, their service was spent mostly in outlandish locations, not only in Britain but around the globe. On 1 July 1943, for example, Command personnel strength amounted to 81,949 — of which total 13,712 were WAAF. These were spread as far

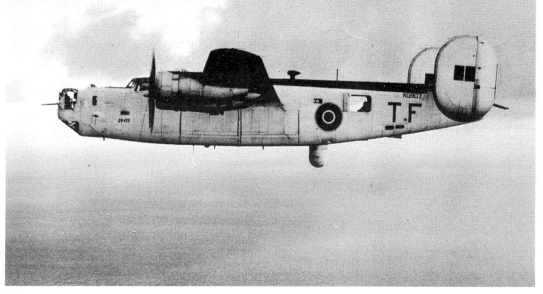

70
Consolidated Liberator GR VI, KG907 from
Aldergrove, with belly radome extended, over the
Atlantic. *W. V. Cluff*

71
The Leigh Light, fitted here to a Liberator, for night
illumination of U-boats. *IWM*

afield as Iceland, the Azores, Gibraltar, West
Africa, and nearer home, Northern Ireland, the
Outer Hebrides, Scotland, Cornwall, Wales,
Lincolnshire, etc. Their tasks were largely
unpublicised, certainly 'unglamorous', and
relatively scantily 'rewarded' in terms of
decorations or other honours. Yet without their
unceasing 'devotion to duty' it is entirely
possible that Britain might not have been
sustained to ultimately play its major part in
defeating Hitler's vainglorious dream of a
'Thousand-Years' Reich'.

AOC-in-Cs, Coastal Command, 1939-45

18 August 1937:	AM Sir Frederick W. Bowhill KCB, CMG, DSO
14 June 1941:	ACM Sir Philip Joubert de la Ferte KCB, CMG, DSO
5 February 1943:	AM Sir John C. Slessor CB, DSO, MC
20 January 1944:	ACM Sir Sholto Douglas KCB, MC, DFC
30 June 1945:	AM Sir Leonard Slatter KBE, CB, DSC, DFC

52

Transport Command

Although the RAF had operated air transportation aircraft for decades prior to the 1939-45 war, these had not been an integral part of any specific organisation tasked solely with this vital role; being mainly undertaken by individual squadrons or other units as circumstances demanded such operations. Prior to 1939, indeed, certain large biplanes had been designated as 'bomber-transport' — a dual role in either of which the aircraft hardly excelled. During 1939-40 the first supplies of Lockheed Hudsons from the USA, ordered on purchase before the war, took a circuitous route from American factory to RAF squadron, often spending up to three months in transit. Following several experimental flights directly across the Atlantic in 1939 the idea of delivering such much-needed American aircraft to Britain by direct air routes bore fruit on 10 November 1940, when seven Hudsons set out from Newfoundland for Northern Ireland and all seven landed safely $10\frac{1}{2}$ hours later. This pioneering flight, led by Capt Don Bennett, BOAC (later AVM, AOC, No 8 (PFF) Group,

RAF), had been undertaken by a mixed batch of Service and civilian volunteer pilots of a recently created Air Ferries Department; an organisation which bore the brunt of trans-Atlantic direct air deliveries of American Hudsons, Fortresses, Catalinas and Liberators over the ensuing eight months.

By July 1941 the introduction of the USA Lease-Lend Act meant that USAAF crews were able to ferry American aircraft direct from the US factories to Montreal, from where they could fly to Britain. In order to 'regularise' this Service ferry system the existing Allied ferrying organisation became retitled RAF Ferry Command, with ACM Sir Frederick Bowhill as its AOC-in-C; the actual Canadian facets of this Command comprising No 45 Group, with two wings — No 112 for the north Atlantic route, and No 113 for the south Atlantic run. By then other transport groups were in existence as well, such as No 216 in the Middle East, and No 179 Wing in India. All worked hand in glove with the civilian-manned British Overseas Airways Corporation (BOAC). The need for plentiful air crews to ensure uninterrupted deliveries from the bountiful American factories was resolved by Bowhill in an imaginative fashion. Since many thousands of future RAF air crews were then being trained

72

DH Albatros AX905, BJ-W, 'Franklin' impressed into service with 271 Sqn 1940.

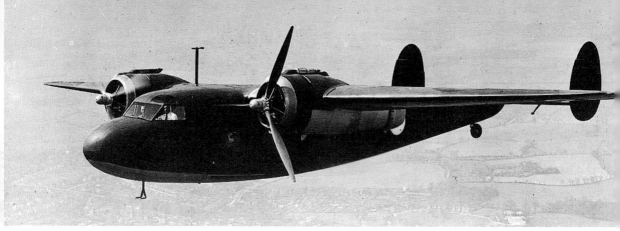

73
Another civil impressment, the DH Flamingo, several of which served with 24 (VIP) Sqn.

in Canada and the USA, why not use these, on graduation, to deliver new aircraft to Britain? Bowhill's idea was accepted and many crews, their recently awarded 'wings' still shiny bright on tunics, found themselves undertaking trans-ocean flights in unfamiliar aircraft, with the not inconsiderable thought that at least they would be back in Britain within hours, rather than suffering weeks at sea via the normal repatriation methods. That this scheme

was highly successful can be judged by the casualty rate — an average of 1% at most.

By mid-1942 Ferry Command, in conjunction with BOAC and several Commonwealth civil air lines, had spread its spiderweb of 'regular' ferrying and supply routes virtually around the globe, flying in total at

74
British Overseas Airways Corporation (BOAC) shared much of the transport role throughout the war, often utilising ex-RAF aircraft. This BOAC Sunderland is viewed at Poole, Dorset in September 1943.

75
The prewar Handley Page Harrow bomber became a useful air transport in the early war years. This modified Harrow BJ-B belonged to 271 Sqn.

least 60,000 hours per month in every known type of aircraft. In addition its British Group, No 44, included a crew-training organisation. On 19 February 1943, acknowledging both the importance and existing strength of the overall RAF transport organisations, the Air Council reviewed all factors and, on 25 March that year, brought all such elements into a new structure titled Transport Command, with the very capable ACM Bowhill as its AOC-in-C. Thus the new Command initially comprised Nos 44, 45 and 216 Groups, and the Indian-based 179 Wing. Expansion of the Command continued apace and by early 1945 the Command had added two new groups, Nos 46 and 47, to the UK-based organisation, and No 229 in SEAC. By then the Command 'owned' 36 stations globally, interspersed by 100 staging posts. Its principal task of ferrying new aircraft to the various theatres of war accounted for such deliveries of some 6,000 machines of many types to Britain, and a further total of more than 3,000 to the Middle East from July 1941 to August 1945 alone. Among the Command's other duties was the highly responsible role of transporting VIP and VVIP (Very & Very, Very Important Personnel) such as royalty, heads of states, senior military, naval, air force and political people around the world; many of whom were specifically air-transported by No 24 Squadron, the RAF's traditional 'VIP Ferry' unit.

If such various forms of flying appeared to the layman as reasonably safe occupations during a war, the Command was not confined to mimicking BOAC, but played its full part in the 'shooting war' too. Principally, its multitudinous flights 'in anger' concerned the transportation of the various forms of airborne troops directly into any required battle zone — ventures fraught with danger for totally unarmed, undefended aircraft and crews. One of the most outstanding such airborne operations occurred in September 1944 on Operation 'Market-Garden', the Allied attempt to secure Arnhem behind the German army's front lines. In co-operation with No 38 Group (administered, curiously, by RAF Fighter Command then), No 46 Group, Transport Command and equivalent USAAF transports carried out airborne operations over nearly a week, daily, beginning on 17 September. On the third day, 19 September, Flt Lt David Lord DFC of No 271 Squadron, flying a Dakota filled with resupply ammunition panniers, had one engine and wing set on fire as he commenced his first dropping run. Turning at the end of this run, still ablaze, Lord deliberately commenced a second run-in through intense anti-aircraft fire to release the last panniers, only to have his Dakota disintegrate, killing all the crew except his navigator. Lord was later awarded a posthumous Victoria Cross — the sole Transport Command recipient of this supreme award for valour. Once the ill-fated Arnhem venture had been abandoned Nos 38 and 46 Groups totted up the collective 'cost' — 55 aircraft lost, with a further 320 damaged by German groundfire and seven by Luftwaffe fighters.

Nos 38 and 46 Groups co-operated again for the massive Allied advance over the Rhine on 24 March 1945 by towing a total of 381 Horsa and Hamilcar gliders containing the British 6th Airlanding Brigade and supporting troops of

76
Douglas C-47 Skytrain *Anabel Lee*, carrying Red
Cross and parachutes' insignia.

77
'Convert' Short Stirling V of 196 Sqn, 1945.

the 6th Airborne Division. The transport crews
achieved a 92% success rate in 'delivering'
their charges in the correct landing zones, but
lost seven aircraft shot down, 27 air crew
personnel killed, and had 32 aircraft damaged.
Thereafter, as the Allied armies and the RAF's
2nd TAF plunged deeper into Germany the
transport crews maintained a constant air
resupply of petrol, oil, ammunition and a
hundred other necessities; No 46 Group alone
dropping some 7,000 tons of supplies in the
month of April 1945. By then, with the collapse
of Hitler's Reich imminent, the two groups,
Nos 38 and 46, had begun repatriating Allied
casualties and released prisoners of war back
to Britain; transporting some 27,000 Allied
prisoners and nearly 6,000 casualties in April
and early May 1945.

Balloon Command

The use of a balloon 'barrage', ie a floating 'carpet' of inflatable kite balloons trailing long wire cables at specified altitudes as an aerial 'umbrella' above vital industrial centres or key cities, had first been used fairly extensively in Britain during World War 1, mainly to protect London from marauding Gotha bombers-*et al*. Its value as a 'deterrent' had been minimal, and continuing experiments during the 1920s and early 1930s confirmed the limitations of any such aerial cover, leading to the conclusion that any such 'barrage' would be best employed at an altitude of approximately 5,000ft with a 'density' sufficient to discourage attempts by any enemy aircraft at low-level or dive-bombing tactics. Accordingly, in mid-1936 the Committee of Imperial Defence approved a suggestion for a 'barrage' of 450 balloons to be installed for the defence of London as the initiation of an eventual national balloon defence organisation. This was to be achieved under the aegis of the Auxiliary Air Force, ie manned by non-regular volunteer personnel, and on 17 March 1937 the first Balloon Barrage Group, No 30, was formed, commanded by a retired RAF officer, Air Cdre J. G. Hearon CB, CBE, DSO, and this formation came under the overall operational control of Fighter Command.

Further expansion soon led to the separate inauguration of Balloon Command, which came into existence on 1 November 1938, with AVM O. T. Boyd CB, OBE, MC as its first Air Officer Commanding (AOC). The new Command remained within Fighter Command's operational control and by early 1939 a total of 47 Balloon Barrage squadrons were in existence, Nos 901 to 947 inclusive, organised basically on a county Territorial system of affiliation. By the outbreak of war in September that year, of an approved establishment for a total of 1,450 balloons considered necessary,

only 624 balloons existed, and 444 of these were based in the greater London area. Initial war production of balloons amounted to 212 in the month of September, and fell to 148 in October, but the urgent need to reach full establishment and eventual expansion soon trebled such production output. Thus, by mid-May 1940, Balloon Command finally achieved its *pre*-war establishment for balloons, but by then was facing the prospects of an imminent occupation of France by German forces. An obvious need for swift reinforcement of anti-aircraft defences of such vital centres as London's docklands and other ports and harbours in south England led to the inclusion of water-borne barrage balloons, either tethered to barges or carried aboard merchant ships. The factory response was intense, with monthly balloon production escalating rapidly towards an intended figure of 1,200, and by 1 August 1940 Balloon Command possessed an actual total of 1,466 balloons spread nationally among 52 operational squadrons, with two more squadrons in the process of being formed as mobile units. This figure compared reasonably with the paper establishment for a total of 1,865 balloons. On that date the Command was organised into five groups:

No 30 Group: London
No 31 Group: Birmingham
No 32 Group: Romsey
No 33 Group: Sheffield
No 34 Group: Edinburgh

The operational value of the balloon barrages throughout 1939-45 was not easily recognised. Certainly, the floating porcine 'umbrella' offered some psychological comfort to the civilian population in bomb-battered towns below, but in practical operational terms its presence often provided as many hazards for

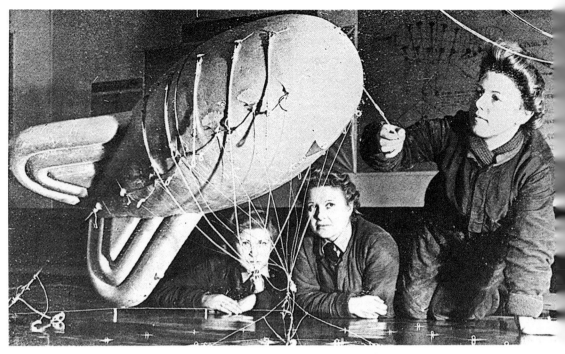

78
WAAFs learning the rigging and tethering of a
balloon via a scale model.

79
Barge-borne balloon for protection of key ports and
river estuaries. *IWM*

the 'defenders' as those met by the 'attackers'. Rogue balloons — those snapping their cables etc and thereafter floating uncontrolled around specific air spaces — were by no means uncommon, while the sheer labour and frustrations of attempting to maintain a balloon 'defence' for some of the outlying naval anchorages, eg in Scotland, amounted to a mini-saga of determination by the balloon ground crews on occasion. Nevertheless, a few individual balloons actually claimed victims among the Luftwaffe invaders of the UK sky; in February-March 1941 at least seven German aircraft being brought down due to hitting balloon cables. From mid-1941 the pace of German air assaults against the UK diminished steadily, but the balloon barrages remained to become a familiar sight around Britain, and proved to be a useful deterrent to many of the hit-and-run sneak attacks by Luftwaffe fighter-bombers along the southern coasts of England during 1941-42.

The next major use of the airborne balloon fleet came with the build-up of Allied forces along southern England in late 1943 and early 1944 preparatory to the Allied invasion of Normandy in June 1944. The vital secrecy of this build-up of strength in such unprecedented quantity meant that every possible measure was needed to prevent Luftwaffe reconnaissance aircraft discovering evidence of these forces, and the balloon barrages played their small but important part in that aerial cover. Then, shortly after D-Day, began Germany's V1 robot flying bomb attacks on southeast England. Again, the balloon barrage became an integral facet of the RAF's defences against this latest example of Teutonic 'hate'. By 29 March 1945, on which day the final V1 fell on Britain, nearly 4,000 'malignant robots' had been brought down by the UK defences, of which total at least 231 were credited to the balloons; a modest proportion perhaps, but the equivalent of possibly several thousand lives being saved apart from any material destruction. The V1 campaign had seen the bulk of the UK's balloon defences concentrate around the south-eastern approaches to England — almost 2,000 balloons by August 1944 — and these had been controlled by the Barrage Commander (sic) in an operations room established at Biggin Hill.

80
WAAF winch-operators being taught the intricacies of a winch mechanism.

A single balloon normally required a team of two Corporals and 10 airmen to maintain it operationally round the clock on a shift-working basis. In 1940, however, the Air Ministry investigated the possibilities for WAAF

airwomen substituting for airmen as balloon operators, despite the protests of AOC Balloon Command and his WAAF Staff Officer at the time. In April 1941 20 WAAF Balloon Fabric Workers, all volunteers, underwent a training course in London, and a month later the first batch of WAAF volunteers was posted to a balloon centre for a 10-week training course and proved highly competent in their new trade. Thereafter WAAF substitution rose rapidly, first on a scale of 20 WAAF substituting for 10 RAF, but eventually replacing men in the ratio of 14 to nine. By the end of 1942 no less than 15,700 WAAF balloon operators had replaced at least 10,000 airmen, releasing the latter for others duties and trades. In January 1943, when Balloon Command was considerably reduced in size temporarily, large numbers of WAAF operators were declared redundant in their trade and 'diverted' to other duties, and further substitution ceased. The WAAF trade of Balloon Operator (Group II) was finally declared obsolete in 1944.

On 5 February 1945 Balloon Command was officially disbanded, and though a number of balloons and their crews continued in service these served in other Commands thereafter. In a sense the Command, which had originally been raised from men of the Auxiliary Air Force, had come full circle, because its last AOC was AVM W. C. C. Gell DSO, MC, and ex-AAF officer. If the men and women who had manned the balloons might be thought to have had an 'easy' war compared with other RAF ground crews, it should be remembered that many had literally served in a 'front line' situation on occasion, particularly so during the 1940-41 period in south-east England where they were subjected to aircraft and long-range German shell attacks. Moreover, no few balloon sites had been in utterly remote corners of the United Kingdom, bereft of all but the barest traces of 'civilisation' and material comforts, and subjected to the wildest extremes of UK weather conditions. As the time-honoured cliche says, 'They also served . . . '.

Photo-Reconnaissance

By 1939, in pursuance of its army C-in-C's edict that, 'The military organisation that has the best photographic intelligence will win the next war', the German Luftwaffe possessed sufficient photo-recce units and personnel to account for almost one-fifth of its overall establishment. By contrast, the RAF at that time had no form of photo-recce organisation at all, beyond an Air Ministry department of Air Intelligence which, in 1938, inaugurated the co-ordination of RAF photo-intelligence, despite the simple fact that the RAF had no firstline aircraft designed for photo-recce work *per se*, or any units designated for such a specific role. In the event this situation was to prove ironic. Whereas the RAF slowly built up an integrated inter-Service photo-recce organisation which played no small part in the ultimate defeat of Hitler's Reich; the Luftwaffe, adhering to its constant tactical application only of air power, failed to take any real advantage from its peacetime organisation of air intelligence until it was far too late to have

any significance. In summary, from the outset, albeit initially in piecemeal fashion, the RAF viewed the whole subject of air intelligence on a strategic level primarily; whereas the Luftwaffe continued to use its photo-recce resources for purely tactical purposes, segmented and unco-ordinated.

In 1938-39 the RAF mainly regarded airborne cameras as merely additional, if useful, appendages to any aircraft's normal war equipment; while the existing Army Co-operation squadrons with such 'specialised' aircraft as Westland Lysanders and Hawker Hectors were thought sufficient for RAF/Army co-ordination of any camera-gathered intelligence purposes. Accordingly, at the outbreak of war most photo-recce operations were simply added to the responsibilities of the Blenheim squadrons of No 2 Group, Bomber Command, despite the overt unsuitability of the standard Blenheim IV bomber for such a role. Of the first 48 Blenheim recce sorties of the war, eight aircraft were lost, while eight other sorties failed to bring back photographs due mainly to weather conditions. Fortunately for the RAF a civilian, Sidney Cotton, working under the aegis of a British Intelligence agency, had spent many hours in 1938-39 flying his own civil aircraft over Germany in the guise of 'business', and secretly obtained excellent photos of many German airfields, fortifications, etc with privately-installed cameras in his Lockheed 12a; and in late September 1939 Cotton was given command of a tiny, highly secret photo-recce unit based at Heston, administered by No 11 Group, Fighter Command. Cotton promptly demanded two Spitfires, had these 'cleaned up', ie gutted of all armament and other superfluous equipment, given a high-speed external paint finish and modified to accept fixed cameras. With additional fuel capacity, the finished 'PR'

82
Spitfire PR VII, X4786 in May 1943. Note camera aperture behind canopy.

Spitfires had a top speed of nearly 400mph, while the nominal range had been extended from some 400 miles to 1,500-1,800 miles. PR Spitfire operations began in November 1939, and after just 15 sorties the Spitfire pilots had photographed twice the acreage of territory covered by 89 Blenheim sorties — and without a single aircraft loss.

Officially titled as Photographic Development Unit (PDU) — though more commonly nicknamed 'Cotton's Circus' — the photo-recce sorties continued throughout the 'Phoney War' and its subsequent blitzkrieg period of May/June 1940, still without any casualties, but when Cotton returned from France he was succeeded in command of the PDU by Wg Cdr Geoffrey Tuttle DFC, and on 8 July 1940 the unit was retitled as Photographic Reconnaissance Unit (PRU), and on 27 December moved its base from Heston to Benson, Oxfordshire. The overall problem of official 'parenthood' was resolved in June 1940 when the PDU had been placed under the operational control of Coastal Command HQ. By the autumn of 1940 the PRU's strength had grown to 11 PR Spitfires, a few Lockheed Hudsons, and miscellaneous communications 'hacks', and Tuttle split these into four (eventually five) detached PR Flights, based at Wick and St Eval, with the remaining aircraft at Heston, then Benson.

From 1940 the PRU came to be used particularly for photographing bomb damage at targets visited by Bomber Command. The photographic evidence thus produced soon proved that Bomber Command crews were

failing to justify any optimistic claims for great destruction in Germany — an issue with no bearing on the PRU's purposes — but also produced the beginning of an ever-increasing accumulation of target photo-intelligence at the Photographic Intelligence Unit (PIU); a central 'library' of such material which gradually offered Bomber (then other) Commands with a wealth of information vital to planning of future raids. In July 1941 the PRU began receiving its first examples of the DH Mosquito PR design, and by September had begun PR operations on the type. The early versions of the PR Mosquito offered a ceiling of at least 35,000ft, a range of 2,000-plus miles, and a maximum speed close to 400mph — the latter 'bonus' being vitally important in any unarmed PR aircraft. By late 1942 it had become increasingly obvious that the PR Spitfires were vulnerable to the much-improved Luftwaffe defences, and in early 1943 the Air Staff proposed that PRU strength in future would be aimed at a 90% Mosquito establishment. In the event a compromise was adopted, whereby the PRU was equipped in roughly equal proportions by Mosquito PR IXs and Spitfire PR XI variants; a 'partnership' which endured throughout the rest of the war.

By June 1943 the still-expanding PRU organisation, including by then the USAAF's 7th Photo Group, was wholly amalgamated under the single title of No 106 PR Wing, still under the administrative control of Coastal Command but in the operational context serving various 'masters'. In May 1944 the wing's status and importance was emphasised when it was 'married' to the Allied Central Intelligence Unit to become a full group; still under the aegis of Coastal Command for paperwork but by then virtually a 'free-lance' organisation in matters of tactics, routine and general employment. By early 1944 the PRU's central processing and interpretation services at Medmenham could provide a veritable computer-style feast of air intelligence for all Services to aid their planning for the Allied invasion of France in June; a 'service' it was to maintain in the highest quality until the end of the European war.

From 1940 the value of photographic reconnaissance had been extended to the Middle East theatres of war, commencing in Egypt and North Africa, then Malta, and eventually reaching along the length of Italy and across the width of southern Europe. For a beginning, No 2 PRU (Benson being numbered No 1 PRU

83
Mosquito PR XVI, MM366 of 60 Sqn SAAF in the Middle East. The rear fuselage striping was an attempt to avoid attacks by 'friendly' USAAF fighters ... *Lt-Col O. G. Davies SAAF*

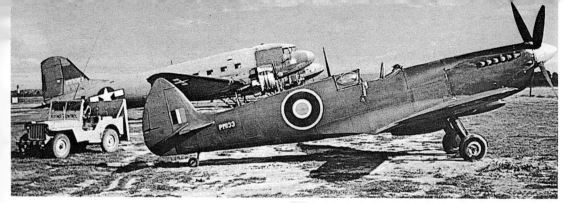

84
Spitfire PM133 in PR blue finish at Eschborne, Frankfurt in 1945. *R. Snyder*

85
Mosquito PR XVI of 140 Sqn, 2nd TAF at Melsbroek, March 1945. In background, a Spitfire PR XI of 16 Sqn. *Fox Photos*

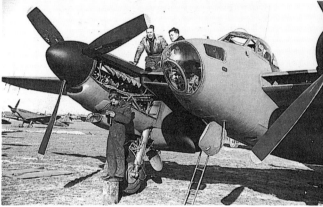

accordingly) was formed at Heliopolis in March 1941, close to Cairo, though a PR element had already existed in Egypt for almost a year by then. PR Spitfires were intended as eventual equipment but in the interim a motley mixture of Hurricanes and Marylands sufficed. Three Marylands had been in use on Malta since August 1940, titled No 431 Long Range Reconnaissance Flight but employed on various duties apart from photo-recce sorties; a unit which eventually became No 69 Squadron, numbering among its pilots Adrian Warburton DSO, DFC, one of the greatest PR pilots ever to serve in the RAF. In the Middle East, as in most operational zones of war, the Spitfire and, especially the Mosquito proved the most efficient aircraft for PR work.

In the Far East theatre PR was not catered for beyond a few individually modified standard bombers or fighters until after the conquest of Malaya by the Japanese, and the first Far East CIU was created in India in March 1942. Then, starting with a mixed bag of Hurricanes and B-25C Mitchells, No 5 PRU was 'born' in April, though this title was amended to become No 3 PRU in May 1942. In October that year, however, the first pair of PR Spitfires arrived on 3 PRU, based at Dum Dum airfield, and by January 1943 the much-expanded unit was again retitled, this time becoming No 681 Squadron. On 9 August two Mosquito PR IIs arrived at Dum Dum, followed by Mosquito IVs a month later, and Mosquito PR sorties began in October. In November 1943

five of Dum Dum's Mosquitos, plus four B-25 Mitchells, became the embryo No 684 Squadron; both squadrons being controlled by No 171 PR Wing, which itself was 'merged' with the USAAF's 8th Photo Group in February 1944 to form the Photographic Reconnaissance Force (PRF). From then until the final Japanese surrender in August 1945 the relatively small SEAC PR Force provided virtually a complete photographic 'map' of Burma, Malaya, Siam, and dozens of other territories; intelligence of supreme importance to the Allied forces advancing through Burma.

In the context of aerial operations the role of the PR pilot was almost unique in 1939-45. The key word was individuality — one pilot, one, unarmed aircraft, alone in hostile skies, facing the myriad hazards of enemy opposition, weather conditions, extremes of temperature, and without any hope of assistance should any of these 'opponents' strike without warning. Unlike the fighter or bomber crews, who — speaking entirely objectively — were 'expendable' once they had attacked their targets, the PR crews' efforts were valueless unless they returned with their 'evidence in camera'. Theirs was possibly the loneliest role of the air war.

Middle East

The term 'Middle East Command', though commonly used, was a somewhat misleading title for a vast area of RAF responsibilities including all RAF units located in or near Egypt, Sudan, Palestine, Trans-Jordan, East Africa, Aden, Somaliland, Iraq, Cyprus, Turkey, Yugoslavia, Rumania, Bulgaria, Greece, countries around the Persian Gulf, the Red and Mediterranean Seas, and other outposts of British colonial and mandated 'control', or 'interests' — geographically, an overall area of almost five million square miles, and larger than the United States of America in such a context. While the RAF had maintained a presence around the Mediterranean zones for some two decades prior to 1939, the Service's actual strength there had never been large, while the Command remained low on the priority lists for modern aircraft and associated equipment. On the outbreak of war in Europe in September 1939 RAF Middle East was commanded by an AOC-in-C, ACM Sir William G. S. Mitchell KCB, CBE, DSO, MC, AFC, who commanded a total of merely 20 squadrons; half of these based in Egypt and Sudan, and the remainder scattered further afield. On 13 May 1940 Mitchell was succeeded as AOC-in-C by ACM Sir Arthur Longmore GCB, DSO, who, when Italy declared war on Britain on 10 June 1940, had a Command comprising 29 squadrons with approximately 300 firstline aircraft plus a 'reserve' of almost 300 more aircraft in 'stock'. Of those 29 squadrons, 14 were designated as bomber units (nine of these equipped with Blenheims); while the only fighter units, five squadrons, were all flying Gladiator biplanes. The remaining squadrons offered a dismal mixture of obsolescent or obsolete biplane designs, or outdated monoplane transport and reconnaissance types.

By January 1941 the Command organisation structure was:

HQ RAF Middle East
(1 Sqn)

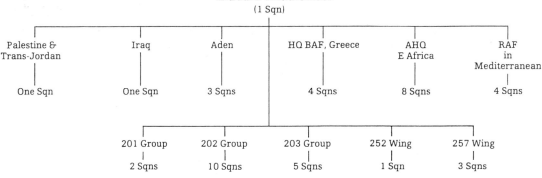

From June to October 1940 the RAF's only opponent was the Italian air force, but on 28 October Italy launched an invasion of Greece and Longmore was ordered to dilute his already meagre air stength by detaching five squadrons to Greece to support the Greek army. His remaining squadrons were then expected to fully support an Allied advance along the North African coast, provide long-range bomber support operations to the Greek

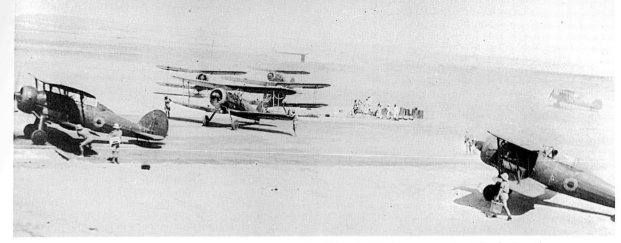

86
Gloster Gladiators of 80 Sqn at Amriyah, early 1940.

struggle from Malta and Egypt, and defend the vital Suez Canal waterway; all this with little immediate prospect of reinforcements from the UK which at that time was still engaged in the latter stages of the Battle of Britain *et al*. In early 1941 the overall situation around the Middle East worsened swiftly from the Allied viewpoint, when German forces began reinforcing their Italian Axis 'partners' in North Africa, invaded Bulgaria, and eventually entered the Greek campaign. The consequent diversification of Longmore's slender air resources could have only one ultimate result, and by mid-1941 the remnants of all the Greek units had returned to Egypt. The only success had been in the East African campaign against the Italians which had, by April 1941, been concluded, thereby releasing some air forces for the greater struggle in North Africa.

By May 1941, however, the Allied situation in the Middle East was gloomy. German and Italian troops stood along Egypt's west borders, were investing Greece and Crete, besieging Malta — the strategic key to disruption of General Rommel's Afrika Korps' reinforcement from Sicily — while a pro-Axis revolt in Iraq, later boosted by German support, threatened Allied access to Iraqi and Persian oil resources, apart from posing the possible further threat of Axis invasion of Egypt for that quarter. In May too German forces began to occupy bases in Syria precipitating an eventual Allied campaign by air and land which resulted in Allied occupation by mid--July. By then Hitler had directed a large proportion of his forces to an invasion of Russia; a move which to some extent provided the Middle East with a measure of stability and permitted a gradual build-up of Allied air strength to oppose Rommel in North Africa primarily. By November 1941 the RAF in the Middle East had grown to the following strength and disposition:

HQ RAF Middle East
2 Sqns

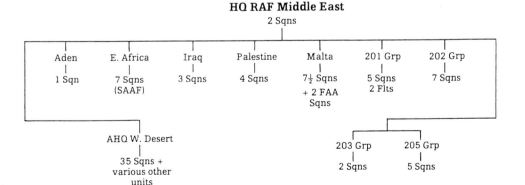

Aden	E. Africa	Iraq	Palestine	Malta	201 Grp	202 Grp
1 Sqn	7 Sqns (SAAF)	3 Sqns	4 Sqns	7½ Sqns + 2 FAA Sqns	5 Sqns 2 Flts	7 Sqns

AHQ W. Desert

35 Sqns + various other units

203 Grp	205 Grp
2 Sqns	5 Sqns

87
Martin Maryland of 60 Sqn SAAF, Egypt, one of several American designed aircraft used by the Allied air forces througout the Middle East campaigns. *Lt-Col O. G. Davies*

88
As in virtually every war theatre, the Hurricane provided the initial backbone of fighter operations. This example, Mk I, BD930, being retrieved from the desert for repair, was with 73 Sqn, and wears the blue (centre) and yellow markings of that unit. *IWM*

89
The Axis air siege of Malta produced desperate combat of an intensity often considered higher than the 1940 Battle of Britain. The island's defenders are represented here by a Spitfire V of 185 Sqn, in its locally improvised dispersal pen.

By that month the RAF could count a total of some 600 firstline, available aircraft for the North African campaign alone.

The period 1941-42 saw a continuing saga of struggle and shifting fortunes in North Africa, as the land armies swayed eastwards and westwards, but also witnessed the escalation of the Axis air forces' attempts to 'neutralise' Malta, which island underwent its severest trials of daily, massive air bombardment and deprivation. It was also a period in which the RAF commander, Arthur Tedder, was able to reorganise and slowly reinforce his squadrons; albeit while continuing to provide continuous air defensive and offensive support to the British Eighth Army and the Commonwealth land forces. From the night of 23 October 1942 — the opening of the Alamein battle and Allied offensive — however, the RAF's clear air superiority over the Luftwaffe in Africa became evident, enabling the Allied armies to advance westwards with escalating success; an offensive which soon became a continuing pursuit of Rommel's troops all along the Libyan coastline, forcing them back into Tunisia. Then, on 8 November, Anglo-American forces invaded Algiers in Operation 'Torch'; a classic pincer move behind Rommel's armies, which was to prove the final seal on the North African campaigns. Intense fighting continued on both 'fronts' until the eventual German surrender in Tunisia on 12 May 1943. The final triumph in Africa owed much to the RAF and its Commonwealth air force partners for gaining undisputed aerial superiority, but also for the complete air-land-sea co-ordination achieved, the basis of which was to become the key to the ultimate defeat of both Germany and Italy in the remaining war years.

Pausing only to regroup and refurbish, the desert air forces next prepared for Operation 'Husky' — the invasion of Sicily, set to commence on 10 July 1943, with Malta as the main 'jump-off' point for the aerial cover squadrons. Despite heavy combat in the initial stages the invasion troops had secured Sicily by mid-August, and then proceeded with the invasion of southern Italy from 3 September. By that date the overall Mediterranean Air Command had expanded vastly, incorporating many mini-air forces capable of operating almost as separate entities when the need arose to protect and pursue particular Allied land/sea operations. In all, throughout the Command, were nearly 300 squadrons or other

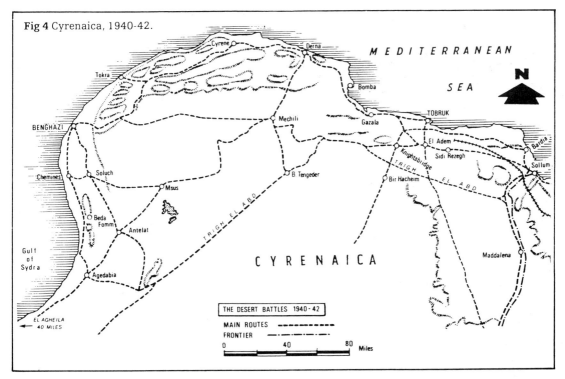

Fig 4 Cyrenaica, 1940-42.

MEDITERRANEAN SEA

Cyrene • Derna • Bomba • Tokra • Mechili • Gazala • TOBRUK • El Adem • Sidi Rezegh • Bardia • BENGHAZI • Knightsbridge • Sollum • Soluch • B Tengeder • Bir Hacheim • Chemines • Msus • Beda Fomm • Antelat • Maddalena • Gulf of Sydra • Agedabia

TRIGH EL ABD

CYRENAICA

EL AGHEILA
← 40 MILES

THE DESERT BATTLES 1940-42
MAIN ROUTES ----
FRONTIER ----

0   40   80   Miles

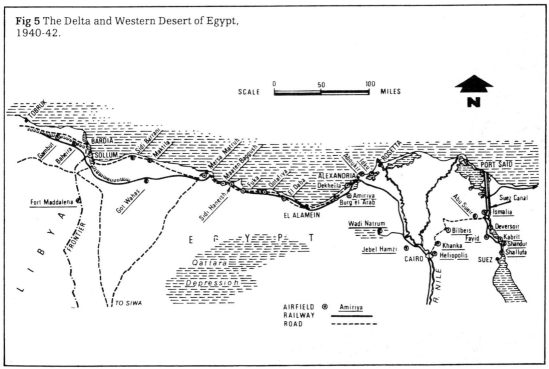

Fig 5 The Delta and Western Desert of Egypt, 1940-42.

SCALE 0   50   100   MILES

N

TOBRUK • Gambut • Bahdra • BARDIA • SOLLUM • Sidi Barrani • Buqbuq • Matruh • Mersa Matruh • Maaten Bagush • Fuka • Daba • Doral'va • El Daba • ROSETTA • PORT SAID • Aboukir • Idku • ALEXANDRIA • Dekheila • Amiriya • Burg el Arab • Suez Canal • Fort Maddalena • Got Wahas • Sidi Hanesh • EL ALAMEIN • Wadi Natrum • Abu Sueir • Ismalia • Deversoir • Bilbeis • Fayid • Kabrit • Khanka • Shandur • Jebel Hamzi • Heliopolis • Shallufa • CAIRO • SUEZ

LIBYA • FRONTIER • EGYPT • Qattara Depression • R. NILE

TO SIWA

AIRFIELD ⊙ Amiriya
RAILWAY ——
ROAD ----

90
The first Spitfires to join the North African campaign arrived in Egypt in May 1942 (two months after the type's arrival on Malta), and first equipped 145 Sqn at Helwan; this pair of Mk Vbs (nearest AB326) being among that first unit batch.

91
Another American design to give trojan service in North Africa was the Boston. Here Boston III of 114 Sqn (pilot, Flt Lt J. Steele, DFC) is pictured in May 1943.

92
Commander of the Western Desert Air Force during the early years was AVM Arthur 'Maori' Coningham, seen here (left) alongside General Alexander at a 1942 Christmas Day service. *British Official*

operational units, including USAAF units which accounted for almost 40% of gross strength, SAAF (18 squadrons), RAAF (7), RCAF (4) and others.

By October 1943 the 8th and 5th Armies had joined in a general northward advance into the heart of Italy, with the air forces in constant close support, providing a new tactical system code-named 'Rover David' and 'Cab Rank' — formations of airborne fighter-bombers able to be called down immediately by RAF liaison officers with the forward infantry elements on

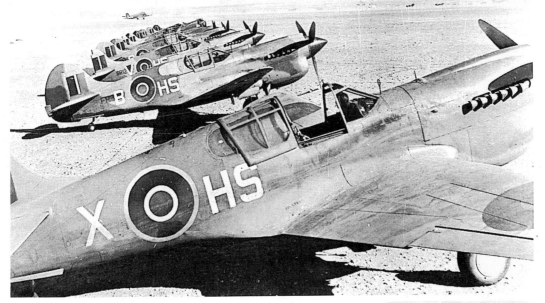

93
Desert 'aces'. Flt Lts Westenra, Neville Duke, and Humphreys of 112 'Shark' Sqn in April 1942 — each displaying the fighter pilot's undone top tunic button. *IWM*

94
Curtiss Kittyhawks of 260 Sqn at an ALG west of 'Marble Arch', North Africa in November 1942. *Wg Cdr J. F. Edwards DFC, DFM*

95
Martin Baltimores over an Italian landscape, 1944 — a design used solely in the Middle East by the RAF, and which first entered operational use there with 223 Sqn in January 1942.

96
Mustang KH774 of 112 Sqn circa March/April 1945 over Italy. *R. A. Brown*

to pinpoint obstacles or targets in the path of the Allied armies. By the close of 1943 the Italian campaign began to bog down as atrocious winter weather conditions prevailed, and a number of squadrons and leading commanders were withdrawn, to be sent either to the Far East, or back to Britain to prepare for the Allied invasion of Europe scheduled for June 1944. During early 1944 further diversion of air efforts involved assistance to Marshal Tito's partisan 'army' in Yugoslavia; support which had been given since the German invasion of Yugoslavia in April 1941 on a slowly increasing scale, and which culminated in June 1944 with the formation of the Balkans Air Force, a 'separate' air force tasked primarily with air support for Tito's quarter of a million guerillas.

By April 1944, with the occupation of the many airfields in the Foggia area, the air forces of the Allies began using these bases for heavy bomber attacks not only in northern Italy but in southern Germany, thereby effectively tightening the 'ring' of aerial bombardment of the Reich in conjunction with the UK-based bombers. On 4 June 1944 Allied armies had taken Rome and were crossing the Tiber in pursuit of a retreating but stubbornly fighting German army; while on 6 June Allied forces invaded southern France, supported by (mainly) USAAF units of the Middle East air formations. The combination of the fall of Rome, the invasion of France, and the escalating air offensive by UK-based bombers against Germany caused most Luftwaffe units to be

withdrawn from the Italian campaign in late 1944, apart from certain nightfighter *Staffeln*. This diminished air opposition left the Allied airmen with virtual air supremacy over the Italian battlefields, and by the spring of 1945 Italian and German ground forces had virtually melted away. On 24 April 1945 an armistice was signed, and on 2 May all hostilities ceased officially. The long hard road from the bald deserts of Africa and Tunisia, across the Mediterranean, into Sicily, then up the entire length of Italy had produced an unchallengeable triumph for the desert airmen. They had also created and epitomised a form of inter-Service integration of common purpose and effort which was to be embellished and executed supremely in the 1944-45 struggle in Europe, and across the globe in the dank jungles of Burma.

AOC-in-Cs, Middle East, 1939-45

1 April 1939:	ACM Sir William G. S. Mitchell KCB, CBE, DSO, MC, AFC
13 May 1940:	ACM Sir Arthur M. Longmore GCB, DSO
1 June 1941:	AM A. W. Tedder CB*
11 January 1943:	ACM Sir W. Sholto Douglas KCB, MC, DFC
14 January 1944:	AM Sir Keith Park KCB, KBE, MC, DFC
8 February 1945:	AM Sir Charles Medhurst KCB, OBE, MC

From 17 February 1943 Tedder became Air C-in-C, Mediterranean Air Command, thereby having operational control over all Middle East air forces, including Malta and NW Africa etc. On 10 December 1943 this Command became Mediterranean Allied Air Forces, absorbing all Middle East and NW Africa air formations.

Far East

The Far East — a generic title for the immense reaches of the Pacific Ocean and land masses stretching from Hong Kong to the sub-continent of India — unlike other areas of the prewar British Empire, was meagerly equipped in terms of air power in the 1920s and 1930s. Until the early 1920s Hong Kong had been regarded as the nodal point of British defence of its Far Eastern outposts of Empire, based on the acknowledged supremacy of the Royal Navy. In 1921, however, it was decided to 'transfer' this key responsibility to the tiny island of Singapore, and plans were inaugurated for an eventual £60 million projected build-up of Singapore as 'the Gibraltar of the Far East' — an 'impregnable fortress', still based on pure naval might. Provision for aerial defence was barely considered initially and even by 1939 amounted to two torpedo-bomber, two light bomber, and two flying boat squadrons — each, with the exception of a handful of modern monoplanes, equipped with obsolete biplanes. Elsewhere in the Far East were a total of nine RAF and one Indian Air Force squadrons; seven of these based in India and equally flying outdated aircraft designs. The collapse of France in June 1940 caused a complete *volte-face* on the part of the Chiefs of Staff in London who met in July, and on 31 July decided that the defence of Singapore must now rest with air power, with a recommendation that the RAF strength should be raised to 336 aircraft by the end of 1941. Despite a further recommendation in October 1940 to increase that figure to 566 aircraft, by December 1941 only 362 aircraft were actually available, and even these were a motley mixture of types, of which 233 could be classified as 'serviceable' for operations.

To accommodate these aircraft, in Malaya generally were no less than 26 'airfields'; four of these on Singapore island itself but 15 of these possessed no concrete runways. Ground defences were almost non-existent, facilities for maintenance and dispersal barely adequate in most cases, while radar 'early warning' installations numbered seven for the whole of Malaya in operative condition. Communication lines were sparse, depending mainly upon the normal civil systems and therefore lacking military security. Such was the command 'inherited on 18 November 1940 when ACM Sir Robert Brooke-Popham took up his appointment as the first AOC-in-C, Far East. By December 1941 — the eve of Japanese invasion — Brooke-Popham's air strength comprised:

Squadron	Aircraft
27	Blenheim IF
34	Blenheim I
36	Vildebeeste
60	Blenheim I
62	Blenheim I
100	Vildebeeste
205	Catalina (three aircraft only)
1 RAAF	Hudson
8 RAAF	Hudson
21 RAAF	Buffalo
243 RNZAF	Buffalo
453 RAAF	Buffalo
488 RNZAF	Buffalo

Total strength in these units was well below 200 firstline, operationally fit aircraft, and no Allied aircraft was any match for the Japanese 'Zero' fighter which was to spearhead Japan's air assaults. The only other air support available to Malaya then were the Dutch Air Force's 22 Martin bombers and nine Buffalo fighters.

On 7 December (or 8th, depending which side of the International Date Line was significant) Japanese forces landed on the beaches at Kota Bahru, while Japanese bombers attacked Singapore city — some 15-20 minutes

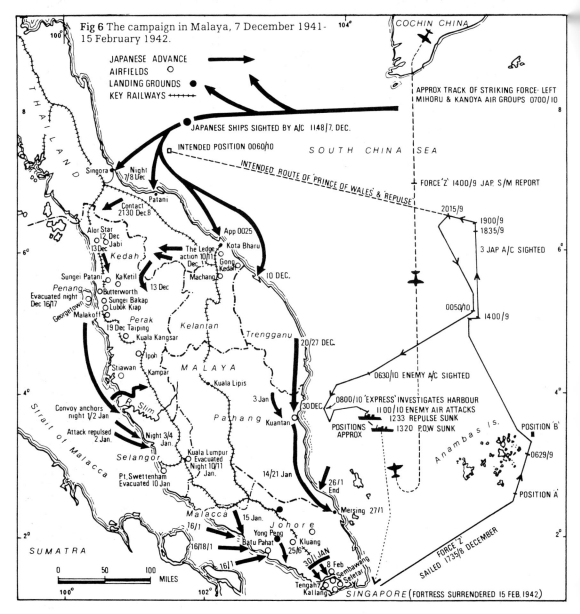

Fig 6 The campaign in Malaya, 7 December 1941 – 15 February 1942.

JAPANESE ADVANCE
AIRFIELDS
LANDING GROUNDS
KEY RAILWAYS ┼┼┼┼┼

COCHIN CHINA

APPROX TRACK OF STRIKING FORCE· LEFT
MIHORU & KANOYA AIR GROUPS 0700/10

JAPANESE SHIPS SIGHTED BY A/C 1148/7. DEC.
INTENDED POSITION 0060/10

SOUTH CHINA SEA

INTENDED ROUTE OF 'PRINCE OF WALES' & REPULSE'

FORCE 'Z' 1400/9 JAP. S/M REPORT

THAILAND

Singora
Night 7/8 Dec
Patani
Contact 2130 Dec.8

2015/9
1900/9
1835/9

3 JAP A/C SIGHTED

Alor Star
12 Dec
Jabi
13 Dec
Kedah
The Ledge action 10/11 Dec
App 0025
Kota Bharu
Gong Kedak
Machang
10 DEC.

0050/10
1400/9

Sungei Patani
Ka Ketil
13 Dec
Butterworth
Penang
Evacuated night Dec 16/17
Georgetown
Sungei Bakap
Lubok Kiap
Malakoff
Perak
19 Dec Taiping
Kuala Kangsar
Ipoh
Kelantan
Trengganu
20/27 DEC.

0630/10 ENEMY A/C SIGHTED

Stiawan
Kampar
MALAYA
Kuala Lipis
3 Jan
30 DEC
Kuantan
0800/10 'EXPRESS' INVESTIGATES HARBOUR
1100/10 ENEMY AIR ATTACKS
1233 REPULSE SUNK
1320 P.O.W SUNK
POSITIONS APPROX

POSITION 'B'
0629/9
POSITION A

Convoy anchors night 1/2 Jan
Attack repulsed 2 Jan.
R Slim
Night 3/4 Jan.
Pahang

Anambas Is.

Selangor
Kuala Lumpur Evacuated Night 10/11 Jan.
Pt. Swettenham Evacuated 10 Jan
14/21 Jan
26/1 End
Mersing 27/1

Strait of Malacca

Malacca
15 Jan.
16/1
16/18/1
16/1
Johore
Yong Peng
Batu Pahat
Kluang
25/6
30/1 JAN
8 Feb
Tengah
Kallang
Sembawang
Seletar

SUMATRA

0   50   100
├────┼────┤
MILES

FORCE 'Z' SAILED 1735/8 DECEMBER

SINGAPORE (FORTRESS SURRENDERED 15 FEB.1942)

before the attack on the American base at Pearl Harbour. Just 71 days later the besieged 70,000 Allied troops in Singapore surrendered to Japanese invasion forces which, by then, had conquered Malaya in toto. In the interim the few RAF units had fought almost fanatically to stem the tide of Japanese incursion, but despite a trickle of Hurricane fighter reinforcements in January 1941, their task was hopeless from the outset, and the last RAF aircraft evacuated from Singapore on 10 February, flying to Sumatra to continue the fight. Here, and shortly after in Java, the Allied airmen fought to a finish, and the survivors were either taken prisoner or managed to make their various ways to India or Australia. Futher north the Japanese had also invaded Burma, seeking the eventual prize of India as their goal. Defending India at the time was a puny force of only 37 aircraft; 21 of these Curtiss P-40s of the American Volunteer Group (AVG), the so-termed 'Flying Tigers'. Against this force

97
The porcine Brewster Buffalo equipped several units in Malaya in 1941 but proved ineffectual against Japanese 'O' fighters.

the Japanese launched some 400 bombers and fighters, attacking first Rangoon on 23 December 1941 with a force of 80 bombers, escorted by 30 fighters. A second such raid on Christmas Day 1941 caused the deaths of 5,000 civilians; but the defending Tomahawks and Buffalos claimed 36 combat victories during the two raids, forcing the Japanese to stop bombing for some four weeks, during which period a squadron of Blenheim bombers and 30 Hurricanes arrived to reinforce India's 'gateway' defenders. Using these to good effect by strafing and destroying Japanese aircraft on their temporary airfields, the air commander, AVM D F. Stevenson, was able to relieve the pressure slightly; while further raids in late January 1942 cost the Japanese a further 100 or more aircraft to Stevenson's fighter pilots.

While the few remaining RAF fighters continued to harass the vastly superior odds facing them on the Indian border, in April 1942 a Japanese naval force, which included five aircraft carriers, attacked Ceylon. This island's

air defences comprised some 36 Hurricanes and six Fleet Air Arm Fulmars, and these claimed 18 Japanese victims during the first air attack on 5 April, but lost 15 Hurricanes and four Fulmars. Further raids gave similar losses on both sides, while at sea the carrier *Hermes* was swiftly sunk by Japanese air onslaught. After sinking a further 14 RN and several merchant ships, the enemy naval force withdrew, but such had been Ceylon's retaliation that three of the five Japanese carriers had to return to base for repair and replacement of their lost aircraft and air crews. While the battle for Ceylon raged, the remaining RAF units in Burma were withdrawn to India to recoup and by the end of May 1942 the initial 'battle of Burma' had ended.

The remainder of 1942 saw the RAF slowly build its air strength. Despite the divergence of many aircraft from Britain to the crucial Middle East campaigns in North Africa, reinforcements trickled through to India, and by July 1942 the RAF in India could count a

98
Curtiss Mohawk II, a fighter which equipped three RAF squadrons in the Far East, 1941-42.

total of 26 squadrons, apart from the eventual eight Hurricane and Lysander squadrons of the rapidly expanding Indian Air Force. At the close of the year an overall total of 1,443 aircraft was available, though many of these were either unarmed transports or non-operational machines. By December 1942, however, these included Beaufighters, first equipping No 27 Squadron, and a few Spitfire photo-recce aircraft, apart from some Wellingtons and Liberators to strengthen the RAF's night-bombing force. In that month the Allies 'leaned forward' for the first time by launching an offensive — the so-termed First Arakan Campaign — to capture Akyab; an offensive which eventually petered out in April 1943. RAF support took the shape (mainly) of destruction of Japanese lines of communication by road and river, apart from fierce opposition to the sporadic attempts by the Japanese air force to intervene. Meanwhile the Army's 77th Brigade (the 'Chindits' as these men came to be titled), under the overall command of Brigadier Orde Wingate, had plunged deep into Japanese-held territory, and were planned from the outset to be supplied with all essentials solely from the air — a tactical ploy which was to become the basic pattern of future years in Burma. For this vital duty the pioneer units employed were Nos 31 and 194 Squadrons, flying Dakotas — a task which each unit carried out with superb expertise and no little courage throughout the whole of the subsequent Burma campaigns.

The continuing strengthening of the Allied air forces brought the British forces' Order of Battle to the following position by June 1943:

Air HQ India (New Delhi)
Air HQ Bengal (Calcutta)

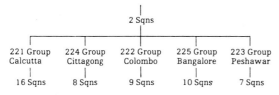

		2 Sqns		
221 Group Calcutta	224 Group Cittagong	222 Group Colombo	225 Group Bangalore	223 Group Peshawar
16 Sqns	8 Sqns	9 Sqns	10 Sqns	7 Sqns

Of this overall total of 52 squadrons, 19 were, for the moment, non-operational, most of which were in the process of re-equipping with more updated aircraft types. Twenty-one of this total were flying Hurricane IIs, a fighter which, if outmoded for firstline operations in Europe and the Mediterranean war theatres,

was to perform trojan work throughout the whole of the Burma 'Forgotten War', 1941-45.

In early October 1943 really 'modern' fighters in the shape of Spitfire Vcs joined the RAF in three squadrons, while more Beaufighter units had been formed or re-equipped, and No 27 Squadron, which had been operating the first two Mosquito aircraft in the Far East since their arrival in April 1943, began re-equipping one of its Flights with the 'Wooden Wonder' in December that year. In November 1943 the expansion of the Allied forces became recognised by a change in overall organisation, with all British and American forces being amalgamated under a new, single operational South-East Asia Command (SEAC). Within this 'marriage' all RAF and USAAF air transport and air supply units became a single formation titled Troop Carrier Command, with Brig-Gen D. Old, USAAF as its first commander. Similarly, both airforces' PRU units combined under a single commander, Wg Cdr S. G. Wise, RAF. By January 1944 two more RAF squadrons arrived, equipped with Spitfire VIIIs, a variant superior to any Japanese fighter and capable of a speed in excess of 400mph and a ceiling of more than 40,000ft.

In February 1944 the Japanese launched a fresh offensive in a bid to capture India, but its initial successes were soon nullified in high degree by two factors. First, the Allied armies refused to retreat, and secondly an unprecedented effort was mounted by the SEAC air services in which they kept up a constant resupply of the jungle-bound soldiers from the air, apart from daring pick-ups of wounded men, while the Hurricanes and Vengeances bombed and strafed every viable Japanese target within range. At the beginning of March the faithful Dakotas airlifted some 9,000 Chindits and their equipment by gliders to deep in Japanese-held jungle some 150 miles behind the fighting 'front', by day and by night — a prodigious feat of airmanship and determination, with scant regard for the myriad hazards involved. By June 1944 the Japanese 15th Army was in retreat, with the ever-present Hurricanes and Vengeances harrying and blasting every point of resistance to the advancing Allied infantry; an aerial 'pressure' maintained throughout that summer's monsoon period. On 1 July 1944 overall Allied air strength showed 100 squadrons, apart from other specialised duty units, with 86 of those squadrons on firstline operations. Further

99
Yet again, the doughty Hurricane gave prominent service in India, Malaya and Burma. This Hurricane IIb, BG827, RS-W, named *Bitsa*, was the 'steed' of Plt Off Jimmy Whalen DFC of 30 Sqn RAF based in Ceylon in August 1942. Whalen was killed in action on 18 April 1944.   *Public Archives of Canada*

100
The aerial 'key' to the ultimate Allied victory in Burma was the dependence of the jungle armies upon resupply by air. The major aircraft used for that 'down the chimney' lifeline was the Douglas Dakota.

101
One of the back-up supply and casualty evacuation aircraft in India-Burma was the Westland Lysander; this example, N1273, BF-J, being one of 28 Sqn's aircraft in 1942.   *B. Robertson*

102
Although used by the USAAF in Britain from 1942, the Republic P-47 Thunderbolt only entered RAF service in the Far East, from May 1944, and eventually equipped nine RAF squadrons. This 'T-Bolt' was flown by Fg Off Terry Marra of 146 Sqn, based at Yelahanka. *Courtesy T. Marra*

reorganisation by then had seen the former Troop Carrier Command disbanded in June 1944, to be succeeded by the RAF/USAAF's combined Combat Cargo Task Force, equipped mainly with Dakotas and C-47s, responsible henceforth for air supplying a third of a million men during the final stages of the Burma conflict. New muscle was added to the fighter-bomber strength by the introduction to Burma of RAF P-47 Thunderbolts, while the ageing Wellingtons were gradually being replaced by Liberators; these latter capable of striking at

Japanese targets, 2,000 or more miles away.

As the 14th Army and its allied armies leap-frogged down the Burmese coastline, recapturing Akyab and Ramree Island *et al*, the Anglo-American air forces moved with them, establishing fresh forward bases from which to maintain their relentless pursuit and destruction of the retreating Japanese armies. During all these operations the patient Dakota crews continued to plod over mountain and valley, delivering the armies' material needs — in February 1945 alone dropping some 60,000 tons of supplies. Such sorties were often made to landing strips in the forward zones under fire from Japanese troops still in foxholes around the perimeters; while elsewhere the tiny, fragile Sentinel L5 'Angels' darted in and out of besieged or harassed Allied positions, their sole mission to evacuate the wounded and sick. By the beginning of April 1945 a 'race' began for the Allies to reach and reoccupy Rangoon before the summer monsoon descended, and in this they succeeded on 2 and 3 May, just hours before the first monsoon rains began. They found Rangoon a deserted city — pounded for a month by Liberator bombing, the Japanese incumbents had already abandoned the city.

There now remained one final major battle in the Burma war — the Battle of Sittang Bend,

103
From early 1944 the Liberator became the RAF's main heavy, long-range bomber in the Far East, both for land bombing and ocean patrols. This Liberator, KG849, 'A' belonged to 203 Sqn.

destined to involve some of the bitterest fighting of the whole campaign. Here some 20,000 Japanese attempted to break free of flanking Allied armies closing in, but between 20 July and 4 August they were to suffer nearly 7,000 casualties. Hurricanes, Spitfires and Thunderbolts kept up a constant 'Cab-Rank' role of flying artillery, bombing, gunning and blasting every known enemy location, and causing an estimated third of the Japanese casualties alone. It proved to be the ultimate fling of an utterly defeated army. Having recaptured Burma, the RAF prepared to implement Operation 'Zipper' — the already-planned reconquest of Malaya — but the USAAF's dropping of atomic bombs on Hiroshima on 6 August and Nagasaki on 9 August nullified any need for 'Zipper'; on 15 August 1945

104
The first Spitfires (Mk Vs) to reach the Far East were delivered in September 1943, but from November that year Mk VIII variants began re-equipping 155 Sqn. The Mk VIII proved superior to any Japanese fighter in the war zone of Burma.
J. H. Farrow

VJ-Day (Victory over Japan) was declared. Within weeks the Liberators and Dakotas were again flying 'maximum efforts' — this time as administering 'angels of mercy' as they began supplying food, medicine and clothing, then uplifting the many thousands of surviving prisoners of the Japanese to centres of succour and comfort. The 'Forgotten War' was over.

AOC-in-Cs, Far East, 1939-45
Air Forces in India

6 October 1939:	AM Sir John F. A. Higgins KCB, KBE, DSO, AFC
26 September 1940:	AM Sir Patrick H. L. Playfair KBE, CB, CVO, MC
6 March 1942:	ACM Sir Richard E. C. Peirse KCB, DSO, AFC

RAF, Far East*
18 November 1940: ACM Sir Robert Brooke-Popham GCVO, KCB, CMG, DSO, AFC

**Strictly, RAF Far East per se had no AOC-in-Cs, but ACM Brooke-Popham's period of appointment, from 18 November 1940 to 27 December 1941, was as C-in-C, Far East, commanding all land and air forces, though not naval.*

Air Command, South-East Asia†
16 November 1943: ACM Sir Richard E. C. Peirse KCB, DSO, AFC
27 November 1944: AM Sir Guy R. Garrod KCB, OBE, MC, DFC
25 February 1945: ACM Sir Keith Park KCB, KBE, MC, DFC

†*Actual title was Allied Air Commander-in-Chief*

Women's Auxiliary Air Force

It is not often appreciated how extensive a contribution the WAAF made to the RAF's overall wartime efforts. The quantitative size of the WAAF alone was remarkable. In May 1943, at which point of the war further entry into the Service was temporarily halted by the Ministry of Labour, WAAF strength stood at some 182,000; while throughout the whole war period approximately a quarter of a million women served in its ranks. In relative strength contexts, the WAAF was 16% of overall RAF strength at the peak of the conflict, and 22% of RAF strength in UK Commands. Considering that the WAAF did not come into official existence until June 1939, and which by September that same year had less than 2,000 members, such escalation in pure members had few equals in any other branch of the RAF apart from the all-male 'preserve' of air crew duties.

The origins of the WAAF may be said to have been in the Women's Auxiliary Army Corps formed in February 1917 to accept women for military duties in non-combat areas 'behind the lines' in France, and (later) in Britain. In November 1917 a similar female service, the Women's Royal Naval Service, came into being for similar duties vis-a-vis the Royal Navy. In addition there was the Women's Legion, a private organisation under the presidency of the Marchioness of Londonderry, which provided a 'corps' of drivers for cars and other vehicles in military formations. All three services, thereby, 'overlapped' with duties directly connected with the Royal Flying Corps and the Royal Naval Air Service. On 29 January 1918 the newly-constituted Air Council agreed, subject to Treasury approval, to the formation of a 'Women's Air Force Corps'; a formation which came into being on 1 April 1918 — the 'birth date' of the Royal Air Force — retitled Women's Royal Air Force.

From that date until 1 April 1920 — the disbandment date of the WRAF — approximately 32,000 women had served in its ranks in Britain, France and Germany.

From 1920-38 a variety of proposals for forming female military organisations were considered but never fully implemented, though the Air Ministry in particular expressed a degree of interest in such a formation relevant to the RAF expansion schemes mooted in the 1930s. By October 1938, however, general agreement had been reached for the inauguration of the Auxiliary Territorial Service (ATS), organised on a county basis under the aegis of the Territorial Army. The ATS was intended to include 'companies' with a particular affiliation to the RAF, and indeed in that same month higher authority suggested that the 'RAF companies' should be affiliated directly to No 601 Squadron AAF and the Balloon Barrage squadrons at Kidbrooke. Further amendments and suggestions for administration and organisation for these 'companies' followed quickly, but finally, in May 1939 the Air Council decided that it would be more desirable to simply form a separate women's service for the RAF, to be titled Women's Auxiliary Air Force. Both Treasury and Royal approval were obtained swiftly, and on 28 June 1939 the WAAF was 'born' officially. The appointment of Miss Jane Trefusis-Forbes as the first 'Director, WAAF' was effective from 1 July 1939, and on assuming her office she was given the rank title of 'Senior Controller', and wore the rank badges of an Air Commodore.

On 28 August 1939, despite an original intention not to mobilise existing WAAF personnel until several months after an outbreak of war, an Air Ministry instruction mobilised them with immediate effect, and authorised recruitment for specific trades. On 3 September

1939, the day war was declared between Britain and Germany, the WAAF comprised 234 officers and 1,500 airwomen, but by 1 January 1940 these totals had risen to 359 and 8,403 respectively. The first WAAF Recruit Depot was established at West Drayton, opening for this role on 30 October 1939. It was by no means a satisfactory location, having been in use as merely an RAF transit camp and lacking most amenities beyond crude accommodation and barely adequate messing facilities, apart from a dreary geographic location during any 'typical' British winter climate. Nevertheless, the enthusiasm of the early volunteer recruits, plus a matching diligence and keenness among the sorely-understrength WAAF staff, overcame most discomforts. West Drayton was to remain the WAAF Recruit Depot until 17 September 1940, when the RAF resumed command in order to inaugurate radar training facilities for airmen, and the WAAF Depot moved to Harrogate, then Bridgnorth, as No 1 WAAF Depot. On 30 December 1940, No 2 WAAF Depot 'opened' at Innsworth as the central reception and training centre for WAAFs in southern England; while No 3 WAAF Depot was inaugurated at Morecambe on 1 October 1941 as a training centre only, but eventually closed as such on 25 February 1943, on which date Wilmslow both received and trained fresh recruits from northern England initially (ie until 15 August 1943, from whence Wilmslow received and trained *all* WAAF recruits).

During the early years of its mobilisation the WAAF found itself in a rather invidious situation. It was not a separate entity as in the case of the ATS and its 'parent' Army, but virtually welded into the skeletal framework of RAF organisation and administration. Yet its members served under a different code of discipline than that firmly established for the RAF. In day to day routine matters, for example, WAAF officers and NCOs had greatly restricted powers of command over any RAF male of whatever rank, yet RAF officers and NCOs had almost full powers over airwomen in work and disciplinary facets. Another, if minor, example of this 'difference' was the fact that exchanges of salutes between WAAF and RAF, at all levels, depended entirely on the individual's code of courtesy, and was not 'enforceable'; this latter aspect remaining so until the close of the war. WAAF administration officers — known officially as 'G' in their title in later years — were regarded by station commanders

105
HRH the Duchess of Gloucester, Air Commandant, WAAF, inspects airwomen of an East Anglian fighter station in early 1941. *British Official*

106
WAAF recruits being issued with their uniforms and kit, 1941. *British Official*

et al as merely advisory 'specialists' in pure WAAF matters, with no laid down executive authority in their own right, and severely restricted in 'action' to those matters considered (by the male senior officer) to be exclusively 'feminine'. A further complication during those early years of the war concerned routine disciplinary powers over WAAF personnel held by either WAAF or RAF officers. Though subject to the Air Force Act (like all airmen) in many routine matters, including civil offences etc, members of the WAAF in 1939-41 could not be charged with the offence of desertion, or absence without leave, due to a short-sighted but legal ruling then by the Judge Advocate General. Nor could *any* disciplinary charge be dealt with summarily, ie within the individual's particular unit, but could only be proceeded with by way of a full court martial, however trivial the offence might have been. Even then, no WAAF officer was permitted to sit as a member of any court martial — under the same JAG's ruling, a WAAF officer was *not* an officer 'within the meaning of the Air Force Act' (sic).

In simple practice this extraordinary ruling meant that any airwoman placed on any disciplinary charge could not be forcibly 'punished' in the normal Service manner, but *had to agree* to be punished appropriately. If indeed the airwoman declined to accept punishment she could simply leave the service without notice, with no possibility of any charge being preferred against her. It was only one facet of an extremely difficult status for the WAAF, but this undesirable situation was eventually resolved by the Defence (Women's Forces) Regulations introduced from 25 April 1941, which declared that all members of the WAAF were members of the Armed Forces of the Crown, and — for one example — Regulation 6 empowered the Air Council to apply the Air Force Act to the WAAF, though with certain sensible modifications and adaptations for specifically feminine items of routine Service life. Despite later attempts to widen the powers over WAAF personnel in the contexts of disciplinary punishments etc, the 1941 decision remained unaltered or extended until the end of the war.

The psychological effect upon long-serving airmen and officers of the RAF in 1939-40 of meeting young girls in the WAAF within what had for decades been an all-male Service community varied widely. In the extremes of reaction were certain senior RAF station com-

107
The Operations Room at HQ Fighter Command,
Bentley Priory in 1940, with WAAF plotters
following each move in the Battle of Britain. *IWM*

108
Ops Eggs. LACW 'Goldie' Goldthorne (centre) waits
to serve 57 Sqn's operational bomber crews with
their traditional 'operational hen-fruit' in the
Officers Mess, East Kirkby.
Sqn Ldr H. B. Mackinnon DFC

109
VIP Chauffeuse. WAAF sergeant MT driver and her
'personal' responsibility. Note 'dim-out' shield on
right-hand headlight. *IWM*

manders who virtually refused to regard any
WAAF seriously in any Service context and displayed an inherent, near-gallant courtesy to all
WAAF, equally and irrespective of rank or job;
while at the other extreme existed a minority of
men who adopted a 'Blimp-like' attitude,
decrying the very notion of women in uniform.
Fortunately, perhaps, the average reaction
from the bulk of airmen and male officers was
one of surprise, amusement, and good humour
initially, which by the close of 1940 had
changed to unfettered admiration and support
from those who had witnessed at firsthand the
superb bearing and coolness, even high
courage displayed by WAAFs who had served
at firstline airfields through the Luftwaffe's
assaults in the Battle of Britain.

These latter girls — for many were still less
than 21 years of age — had remained at their
posts despite strafing, bombing, and scenes of
carnage and horror. Their refusal to quit is all
the more praiseworthy when it is remembered
that (as already explained) each girl had it
within her own decision whether to desert or to
remain among such terrifying conditions. The
original principle for formation of the WAAF
had been one of substitution, whereby airwomen could eventually take the place of
airmen in certain non-combat duties and
trades in order to 'release' able-bodied men for
more 'active' zones and duties. In the beginning
trades 'open' to WAAFs were few. WAAF
officers, in 1939, were appointed solely for
administration duties, while non-
commissioned airwomen could only be
employed in administration, as clerks, become
cooks or kitchen orderlies, equipment
assistants, balloon fabric workers, or drivers of
RAF mechanical transport — virtually all tasks
traditionally associated in the chauvinistic
male's mind as 'suitably feminine' roles. By the
end of 1940, whoever, a total of 18 trades were
open for WAAF 'substitution' including several
technical or mechanical trades; while by
October 1945 women had been successfully
'substituted' in 15 officer categories and 59
airmen trades. Apart from 21 other trades
either created solely for WAAFs or specialised
WAAF trades. The idea of women actually
undertaking air crew operational duty was
never approved (despite the large proportion of
fully competent female pilots employed in
Ferry Command and the Air Transport
Auxiliary — ATA — and Russia's common use
of women as frontline soldiers and operational
air crews). One other embargo resolutely

81

110
Heavy stuff. WAAF tractor driver at the helm of a bomb 'train', about to be delivered to aicraft dispersals.

111
Cpl Vera Carter, a WAAF R/T Operator, at Waddington's 'Patrol Handling Board' (sic) on 12 May 1944, awaiting the return of Lancaster R5868 'S-Sugar' of 467 Sqn RAAF from its supposed 100th operational sortie. In near foreground is the Station Commander, Grp Capt Bonham-Carter. *Central Press*

unchanged was the War Cabinet's refusal to allow women to carry 'lethal weapons' — a somewhat 'blind' judicial 'eye' apparently being applied to the many hundreds of WAAFs employed in armament trades, tractor-driving 'trains' of lethal high explosive bomb loads from bomb dumps to bomber dispersals, *et al*.

Contrary to the somewhat glamorous image of life in the WAAF portrayed both by the media and officialdom in its recruiting propaganda outlets, in practice the WAAF rank and file often faced the same dismal wartime temporary accomodation and lack of 'civilised' facilities and amenities suffered by a majority of male non-commissioned ranks; especially on operational stations or wartime airfields. In deference to traditional custom and contemporary codes of morality, WAAF personnel were, whenever practicable, accommodated, fed, etc separately from equivalent male personnel, but by mid-1943 'mixed' accommodation and messing had begun to be accepted as necessary in the interests of simple economy or plain practical circumstances. In terms of actual pay, the WAAF suffered inequality with their male counterparts throughout the war, being paid (at virtually all levels of rank) roughly two-thirds of the daily rates enjoyed (?) by equivalent airman ranks. This inequality, incidentally, also applied to the bureaucratic scale of ration allowance, whereby an airwoman was accounted as fourfifths of an airman's allowance — the official reasoning being (quote) 'It is well known that women need and actually consume less food than do men' ...! It was not until 1944 that this latter disparity began to be amended to equal ration allowances for WAAF officers and certain WAAF tradeswomen (eg WAAF Balloon operators), but had not been fully implemented by the end of the war.

While most WAAF personnel based in the United Kingdom shared almost equally with their male counterparts in suffering the idiosyncracies and mysterious (to most airmen and airwomen ...) logic of RAF Records Office postings and detachments to far-flung corners of the UK; overseas' postings remained a mainly male 'privilege' throughout the war. Of the total number of women who served in the WAAF from 1939-45, less than 9,000 — or about 4.5% — went overseas, all of these being volunteers. It was not that many WAAF at all rank-levels were unwilling to leave the UK, but simply due to higher authority's appreciation of the many purely practical problems that would

occur abroad. The first WAAF to be posted overseas were three officers in the cypher trade who went to Washington, USA in mid-1940. In 1941 the total in USA, Canada and Egypt rose to 29, all officers; while by July 1942 no less than 149 WAAF officers were stationed in the Middle East zones, with 35 others in the USA, and a further 13 in Canada. Non-commissioned airwomen did not commence being accepted for overseas duty until late 1943, but by July 1944 a total of 1,571 airwomen 'rankers' and 178 WAAF officers were serving in the Middle East; a statistic which had risen to 3,365 and 175 respectively by July 1945. In September 1944, following the Allied invasion of Normandy in June that year, three WAAF officers and 10 airwomen were stationed in France. By July 1945, totals of 63 WAAF officers and 1,451 non-commissioned airwomen were based in France, Germany, or (mainly) Belgium; while in the same month totals of 114 officers and 1,184 airwomen were serving in either India or Ceylon, and 145 others were based as far afield as Bermuda, Bahamas, Labrador, Newfoundland, Norway and Melbourne, Australia.

If any single generic description could be isolated to offer a hint to the quality of the wartime WAAF, it would probably be 'volunteer'. By the close of 1941 a total of 81,928 women had voluntarily enlisted in the WAAF. On 10 January 1942, by Royal Proclamation, single women born in 1920-21 became liable, with rare exceptions, to be conscripted under the aegis of the National Service Act; while throughout that year many

112
Section Officer Mary Russell de-briefing a bomber crew, just returned from Stuttgart.

113
Water-baby. WAAF serving with a Coastal Command squadron attired in protective 'wading' clothing.

hundreds of other women born in the 1918-23 parameters were interviewed for WAAF service as conscription gradually expanded its age groupings. Side by side with this conscription, volunteers for the WAAF by women 'outside' the enforceable age limits continued to appear at recruiting offices, and throughout 1942 totals of 62,091 pure volunteers joined a further 16,246 women in joining, by personal preference, the ranks of the WAAF. By December 1945 the total number of WAAF recruits accepted throughout the whole war showed a gross figure of 217,249, of which a total of 33,932 had enlisted under the terms of the National Service Act in the years 1942-44 and opted to join the WAAF in preference to the Army's ATS and the Royal Navy's WRNS equivalent female Services. While quoting pure statistical strengths, it might be noted that the WAAF reached its peak numerical strength by 1 July 1943, on which date it stood at 181,835 airwomen of all ranks.

In summary, the fundamental object for the existence of the WAAF was to help to ensure that no aircraft was ever grounded because the men who serviced, maintained, or in any way contributed to the ultimate aim of the RAF in 'keeping them flying', were employed in duties often far removed from such supportive roles which could readily be undertaken by women. That the WAAF succeeded so splendidly in fulfilling their prime objective may be judged by the official postwar estimate that *without* the support of the WAAF, the RAF would have required 150,000 extra men to have achieved its final success; men who could only have been forthcoming at the expense of the other fighting services or Britain and the Commonwealth's industrial workforce, to the detriment of each of the latter. Many hundreds of WAAFs were granted honours and awards for gallantry, courage, or other sterling services of a 'non-combatant' nature, but for the vast majority their war service had encompassed many personal hardships and privations, in duties too often dull, monotonous, even servile to some degree, where it was more than often difficult to say the least, for them to see or feel that they

114

LACW Myra Roberts, Cpl Lydia Alford, and LACW Edna Birbeck — the first WAAFs to go to France after D-Day, on 13 June 1944, for air 'ambulance' medical duties.

were doing a 'vital' job, necessary for the overall war effort. That most overcame such natural reservations and continued to give unstinting energy and devotion to their duties in such circumstances merely reflects the generally high dedication of their Service. Wherever WAAF were stationed they always managed to introduce a 'feminine' touch of 'civilisation' to grim, usually stark surroundings, while many an ex-wartime operational air crew will attest to the sheer psychological comfort they derived on return from the hell of an operational sortie over Europe on hearing the soft, cool, feminine voice of a WAAF radio operator in the base Air Traffic Control tower, greeting them and guiding them in over the final lap to a safe landing.

Princess Mary's RAF Nursing Service

The logical corollary of a medical and nursing service attached to any form of fighting formation has roots stretching back over centuries, and when the Royal Air Force came into existence in April 1918 it proved to be no exception, with the RAF Nursing Service being created in June that same year. The RAFNS's initial staff comprised mainly trained Army nurses, and the original establishment was one Matron-in-Chief, four Matrons, and 40 Sisters or Staff Nurses, scattered among station sick quarters at Cranwell, Halton, Uxbridge, Glasgow, Birmingham, Sheffield and Salisbury Plain, and convalescent centres at Matlock, Hastings and Hampstead. By January 1919 the Army nurses had been replaced by regular members of the new Service, and gradually all nursing personnel at the temporary wartime camps were withdrawn to the permanent training stations, notably Cranwell and Halton. Finally, on 27 January 1921, the RAF Nursing Service was officially established under Royal Warrant as a permanent branch of the RAF; while in June 1923, by consent of HM King George V and HRH Princess Mary, the RAFNS was honoured with a new title of Princess Mary's RAF Nursing Service. The first appointed Matron-in-Chief was Dame Joanna Cruickshank DBE, RRC who had under her command five Matrons — stationed at Halton, Cranwell, and the (then) RAF Central Hospital at Finchley — and four Senior Sisters, 25 Sisters, and 85 Nursing Sisters based (mainly) in the UK or more sparsely abroad at Aboukir, Egypt, Baghdad, Basrah, and in Palestine. These overseas hospitals were first founded in Basrah and Hinaidi, Iraq in 1922, followed by Palestine (1924) and Aden (1928).

A further indication of royal patronage and close interest came on 31 October 1927, when HRH Princess Mary, Countess of Harewood, opened the modern hospital and nursing staff quarters at RAF Halton, giving this establishment the royal prefix — the only one so titled. Thereafter Halton remained the principal training station of the PMRAFNS. In January 1930 Miss K. C. Watt CBE, RRC who remained in that appointment until her retirement in July 1943, handing over control to Miss G. Taylor RRC. From 1918 members of the Service enjoyed the status of commissioned officers, but in 1943 actual commissioned ranks were granted, with appropriate equivalent RAF rank badges. Though commonly addressed by their professional titles, these were:

Matron in Chief:	Air Commodore
Chief Principal Matron:	Group Captain
Principal Matron:	Wing Commander
Matron:	Squadron Leader
Senior Sister:	Flight Lieutenant
Sister:	Flying Officer

Their correct Service designation was 'Nursing Officers'.

Prior to, and throughout 1939-45 all members of the PMRAFNS were Registered State Nurses who had served four years at a civil hospital, and were civil-qualified under the regulations of the General Nursing Council, apart from certain personnel qualified in specialised branches of nursing. Trained nurses were eligible for regular service in the age range 23-35, while in wartime eligibility for Volunteer Reserve service only had the extended age range of 22-45 years. Ancillary to the PMRAFNS in RAF hospitals were members of the Voluntary Aid Detachments (VAD), who were addressed as 'Nurses' and wore VAD uniforms, and worked under the supervision of PMRAFNS Sisters in the wards. From early 1940, however, suitably qualified women in the Women's Auxiliary Air Force (WAAF) began

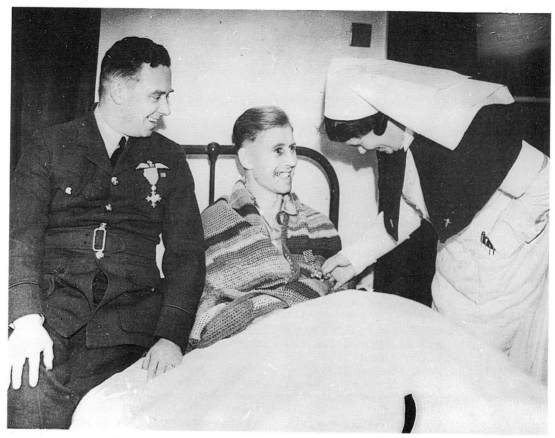

115
A PMRAFNS Sister admiring the DFC awarded to
Flt Lt W. B. Goddard of 235 Sqn, while Plt Off
Westgate is wearing his MBE award. One of the
'Few', Goddard was killed in action later in the
war. *British Official*

serving alongside their male colleagues as
medical officer/doctors, while WAAF non-
commissioned airwomen could enter several
associated medical trades. These WAAFs were
not members of the PMRAFNS, being (then) still
members of an auxiliary (as opposed to regular)
Service, but their frequent presence in medical
establishments throughout the RAF steadily
extended as the war progressed. From 1943
nurses and medical staff of all three Services
(PMRAFNS, VAD and WAAF) began undertaking airborne 'ambulance' duties, and from June
1944 particularly were ever-present on air-

craft ferrying wounded and sick troops to the
UK from the European battle areas.

Although most airmen's and airwomen's
only contacts with the various medical staffs
usually consisted of attendance as an out-
patient for temporary disorders — or the then
mandatory FFI (Free from Infection) inspection
'parade' on return from any spell of leave —
and, when due for overseas' postings, an
armful of 'appropriate jabs' (inoculations
against tropical diseases etc); many thousands
of battle casualties owed their lives to the
skills, resourcefulness, and unending patience
of those same 'angels'. The Halton hospital, for
example, became the RAF's recognised centre
for specialised treatment of burns' cases,
especially air crews of all the Allied air forces,
and this establishment liaisoned closely with
such 'non-RAF' centres as Archibald McIndoe's
legendary 'Guinea Pig' hospital at East
Grinstead.

RAF Regiment

The vital need for ground defence of RAF airfields and other key bases was appreciated almost from the earliest years of the RAF's existence, particularly from the early 1920s when the infant air service began assuming responsibilities for 'control' of various territories, colonies, and mandated countries abroad. The 'seeds' of such a 'defence' force were sown with the creation of Nos 1 and 2 Armoured Car Companies in the Middle East areas in 1921 and 1922 respectively. Over the following two decades these companies provided sterling support for RAF activities operationally, and were to continue their spearhead role throughout the North African campaigns of 1940-43 especially. Another form of ground 'defence' was provided along parallel lines by the various Levies' formations created from 1915 onwards in Iraq (then, Mesopotamia) and, from 1928, Aden. Inaugurated originally as 'bodyguards' for the many British Political Officers administrating overseas territories under British 'control', these British-officered native formations grew into mini-armies who saw plentiful active service in many theatres of the Middle East.

In Britain, however, the need for a force tasked solely with guarding RAF bases from 'enemy' attacks or intrusion, though recognised as desirable in wartime, was not implemented in practice during the post-1918 peace years. In November 1933, however, it was agreed that the RAF would organise its own defences against low-flying air attacks, and the means and methods for doing this continued to be debated for several years. In 1937 the Air Council directed AOC-in-Cs that they were responsible henceforth for 'defence of RAF aerodromes and other air force establishments against low-flying air attacks, and for local defence against attack by land forces . . .'. Impressive as such a directive might have appeared, however, it overlooked the fact that the RAF then possessed no suitable weaponry for such a task, or suitably trained airmen for such specialised duties. Thus when on 2 September 1939 the 10 squadrons of Fairey Battles of No 1 Group, Bomber Command were despatched to France as the AASF, their only base defences comprised 100 .303in calibre Lewis machine guns in the hands of small force of airmen titled Ground Gunners, men in the lowest trade Group V, with only the sketchiest of actual training in their stipulated role, albeit firmly dedicated to their task. When the German blitzkrieg offensive commenced in France and the Low Countries on 10 May 1940, the airfield defence forces available to the RAF in France comprised eight 3.7in, 40 3in and 24 anti-aircraft guns (40mm Bofors) — all manned by Army personnel — plus 433 machine guns of varying types manned by 835 RAF ground gunners. In the event, this 'defence' was overwhelmed and RAF airfields strafed and bombed almost without impediment.

In the United Kingdom then a total of 365 RAF stations were provided with 'anti-aircraft' machine guns — again, merely 1918-vintage Lewis guns in the main — manned by some 3,000 ground gunners trained at RAF North Coates. The machine guns were later supplemented by 376 20mm Hispano cannons. The bulk of the airfield defences remained under aegis of the Army — some 14,000 soldiers providing Light Anti-Aircraft (LAA) defence for 139 of 255 RAF stations defended solely by Army personnel. The patent urgency for the RAF to be capable of defending its own bases led to a Directorate of Group Defence being formed in Air Ministry on 27 May 1940, with Air Cdre A. P. M. Sanders as its first Director.

The Directorate's initial task was to organise and train defence 'forces' already existing on RAF stations, and station commanders were immediately held responsible for co-ordinating all local resources in their particular areas, and were provided with 'specialist defence officers'; these latter being in too many cases elderly retired ex-Army officers vastly outdated in notions of modern warfare, unfortunately.

From July to October 1940 — the official period parameters of the Battle of Britain — the airfield defenders went through a violent 'blooding' in their role as the Luftwaffe concentrated on destroying the RAF's key defence arifields. Their response, in the circumstances, was admirable. Confirmed claims for 15 enemy aircraft actually destroyed and six others seriously damaged may not appear to indicate high success, but the overall deterrent effect on low-strafing enemy aircraft of a virtual barrage of small-arms fire undoubtedly contributed much to the ultimate RAF triumph. In this period too came the first gallantry award to an RAF ground gunner, a Military Medal (MM) to Cpl Jackman for operating his Lewis gun defending RAF Detling until his post was destroyed and he was severely wounded. By the end of 1940 the RAF had some 35,000 men serving as ground gunners and in April 1941 these existing defence personnel began being organised into squadrons, with plans for increasing the number to 72,000. In the follow-

116

General Bernard Montgomery inspecting an RAF Regiment guard of honour in 1943, accompanied by (left) AM Leigh-Mallory. The gunners are in khaki battle dress, with RAF blue berets, patches, and webbing; blue battle dress for the Regiment was not introduced until 1950. *MOD(Air)*

ing month German paratroops led an invasion of Crete, thereby providing the catalyst on airfield defence planning; resulting eventually in a Chiefs of Staff report in June 1941, extended in a further recommendation in November that year that the RAF should form its own aerodrome defence force 'forthwith' under the control of Air Ministry.

The War Cabinet approved this recommendation in December 1941, and in January 1942 announced the impending formation of the RAF Regiment as a specialised airfield defence 'corps'. The Royal Warrant signed on 6 January 1942 declared the RAF Regiment to be 'a Corps formed as an integral part of the Royal Air Force', and Air Ministry Order N.221/1942 stated that all existing defence formations were to be incorporated in the RAF Regiment with effect from 1 February 1942 — on which date the new formation came into being, with Maj-Gen Sir Claude Liardet CBE, DSO 'loaned' from the Army as its first appointed Commandant.

In the UK at that moment were approximately 66,000 RAF defence personnel divided between 150 defence squadrons and 336 defence flights; the squadrons having been given numbers 701 to 850 in December 1941. These were renumbered as 2701 to 2850 as the first official RAF Regiment squadrons and given fresh establishments, while the 'independent' flights were numbered, for the first time, from 4001 to 4336. By the end of 1942 these units had become classified in two main types; Field squadrons, each composed of seven officers and 178 airmen, known later as Rifle squadrons, and Anti-Aircraft Flights comprising each of one officer and 60 airmen

manning 12 20mm Hispano cannons. Within the same year the RAF Regiment was able to provide units to relieve the many Army formations based at RAF airfields in the UK, thereby 'returning' a large number of Army personnel to their parent regiments *et al.* Meanwhile, similar RAF Regiment flights — later, squadrons — were provided in the Middle East theatres of operations to guard outlying staging posts and landing grounds; while the first anti-aircraft flights reached Burma in late 1942, and a Regiment Depot was established at Secunderabad, India to form and train flights for the Burma struggle.

In the North African campaigns of 1940-42, including the 'side-show' operational conflicts in Iraq, Syria etc, the prime defences for the RAF's airfields had been the long-established Nos 1 and 2 Armoured Car Companies, always well to the fore in each advance by the land armies, and receiving well-earned official praise for their doughty and vital prowess. With the advent of the RAF Regiment, higher authority proposed that these companies should be absorbed into the new force, but this was rejected by the Air Ministry and the armoured car companies continued their separate existence and roles until 1946. In November 1942 the RAF Regiment had its first true testing in battle in two Allied advances, when five Field squadrons and five LAA Flights were part of the invasion force which landed in Algiers on Operation 'Torch'; while Regiment guns went forward with the Allied advance from El Alamein, moving ahead of the infantry to occupy abandoned airfields and clearing snipers, booby traps, mines or any other obstacles, human or material likely to impede the Allied advance. They were, for example, the first to occupy El Daba airfield on 5 November 1942. The battle experience gained from these North African campaigns virtually set the future pattern for employment of RAF Regiment squadrons or flights. While ready to relieve any Army personnel in the static airfield defence role, the Regiment was also henceforth acknowledged as an essential element of any Allied spearhead assault formation, able to capture and hold key air strips and prepare them for Allied Air Forces' forward use in any battle or invasion.

On 10 July 1943, for example, two Regiment squadrons landed with the invasion forces on Sicily's beaches, and were supplemented within nine days by four more squadrons. By September a total of 11 Regiment squadrons were in Scily, in fierce action with frontline forces. In that same month another Regiment squadron, No 2906, landed at Salerno alongside the Army on 9 September, followed by more units in rapid succession across the Straits of Messina, moving quickly northwards to capture forward airfields for Allied fighter squadrons. Elsewhere around the Mediterranean zones, RAF Regiment squadrons were involved actively in the Balkans, the Aegean, and in the reoccupation of Greece in late 1944; each unit fighting fierce opposition in a variety of amphibious or land campaigns and battles. Its fighting spirit as an elite corps was perhaps no better exemplified than in September 1943 when the Regiment accompanied the Allied invasion of the island of Cos. Its gunners were in unceasing action from the first day until the island was retaken by the Germans three weeks later, and a Royal Artillery officer who managed to escape from the beleaguered island paid a personal tribute, saying: 'There was a cheery and defiant courage about them and a pride in their Regiment which impressed all. We will always remember them for their unfailing cheerfulness, their utter determination to fight their guns to the very end, and their great courage. We were all proud to know them.'

While their comrades in the Middle East were establishing a superb fighting reputation for the Regiment, the UK-based units were playing an equally vital part in the defence of Britain by combatting the sporadic assaults from the Luftwaffe in 1943, and, in late 1944, the V1 robot flying bomb menace. In early 1943 a number of RAF Regiment units were redeployed from RAF airfields to the south coast of England to tackle the 'hit-and-run' Luftwaffe attacks there; one armoured car flight, No 2892 Squadron, destroying six enemy aircraft alone during a raid on Torquay on 30 May 1943. By early 1944, however, the massive build-up of manpower for the imminent Allied invasion of France — Operation 'Overlord' — provoked a crisis, and the RAF was forced to agree to a reduction in strength to bolster the Army's needs. The result was a dramatic transfer of some 40,000 trained gunners from the RAF Regiment to the Army, but the importance of the force was recognised by the inclusion of no less than 19 wings (ie 38 squadrons) of the Regiment in the initial landing forces; two wings sailing on D-Day, and a further eight wings being on Normandy soil by 18 June (D+12), while by the end of August 1944 a total of 18 wings were firmly established on the Continent. Indeed, a flight of No 2728 Squadron was among the first Allied units to reach and enter Paris on 25 August. These units remained in the vanguard of the advancing Allied armies throughout the subsequent campaigns and battle for France, the Low Countries, and finally Germany itself. Their high effectiveness in action may be judged by the occasion on New Year's Day, 1945 when the Luftwaffe launched its *Bodenplatte* attack on Allied airfields occupied by the 2nd Tactical Air Force. On a total of 11 airfields defended by Regiment LAA units, the gunners shot down 43 German aircraft and at least damaged 28 others. By March 1945 the Regiment's strength in North-West Europe amounted to 65 squadrons. These were used primarily to advance *ahead* of the Army to secure key positions, and in the early days of May nine Regiment 'task forces' moved forward into Schleswig-Holstein and seized 15 airfields, apart from receiving the surrender of some 50,000 German troops; and by VE-Day, 8 May, Regiment strength had risen to 74 squadrons, many of which remained in Europe as part of the Occupation Air Forces.

From June to October 1944 the UK-based Regiment units too were in action, this time as part of the UK defences against the V1 robot flying bombs being showered upon Britain both by day and night. Thirty-one squadrons were sent to southern England between 28 June and 3 July, while at the end of July a further 21 squadrons were 'detached' to defend the Thames Estuary area. The units on the southern coastline manned a total of 584 light anti-aircraft guns, mainly 20mm Hispano cannons, and claimed a fair proportion of successful 'interceptions'.

While the RAF Regiment units battled in Europe, halfway across the globe their counterparts in India and Burma were maintaining the Regiment's high standards of dedication and courage. By late 1944 six field squadrons and 62 LAA flights had been formed, trained, and deployed to firstline duties. As early as June 1943 two field squadrons and 10 LAA flights had been allotted to the Arakan, defending airstrips from Cox's Bazaar to Imphal, and by early 1944 these were concentrated in the Imphal Plain and the Surma Valley fighting zones to protect the RAF's forward landing grounds. When, in March 1944, the Japanese broke into the plain, threatening the security of these airstrips, the

Regiment units fought doggedly against all odds, and by August, when the Japanese finally began their retreat from Burma, the Regiment was, as always, to the fore in advancing; No 2944 Squadron in November 1944 being the first RAF unit to cross the Chindwin River. From then until Japan's capitulation in August 1945 the Regiment units added numerous 'laurels' to their reputation. Merely one example may reflect the overall nature of their 'war'. In early March 1945 the invaluable Meiktila airfield complex was initially captured by four squadrons of No 1307 Wing. Japanese opposition was near-fanatical and continuous over the ensuing 10 days, forcing the Regiment gunners to evacuate the airstrips each night, then refight each morning to enable the RAF's aircraft to utilise these grounds, well behind the so-termed 'front lines'. It was here that one Regiment Sargeant, N. Gerrish, earned a Military Medal for commanding a rifle flight in a night defensive battle with Japanese infantry, despite being wounded early in the clash. Such was his determination that his flight pinned down two Japanese companies, killing a large number of them in the process. His award was but one of dozens gained by individual RAF Regiment officers and gunners throughout the Far East war. Regiment units were again among the first RAF units to reoccupy Singapore and other Malayan cities, Penang, and Hong Kong as the Japanese nation offered to surrender.

By the close of 1945 RAF Regiment units in South-East Asia Command (SEAC) amounted to 33 squadrons, whose indefatigable efforts brought them high praise and well-earned plaudits in the various senior RAF commanders' summary despatches at the close of hostilities with Japan. Their fighting record was second to none, which could equally be said for every other Regiment unit during the three and half years of its existence since original formation. Wherever the RAF had operated during 1942-45 the Regiment had been represented, carrying out virtually every facet of ground combat duties. At its wartime peak the Regiment had numbered more than 85,000 men of all levels in its ranks, and possessed overall some 240 squadrons. Despite its short Service life, the RAF Regiment's proud war record ensured it a permanent place in the postwar regular RAF, and to signify this deserved honour, HM King George VI accepted the appointment of Air Commodore-in-Chief of the Regiment in September 1947.

Air-Sea Rescue and Marine Craft

Although the RAF Marine Branch was not officially formed until 1948, the RAF had employed a wide variety of maritime vessels operationally from its earliest origins. At its 'birth' on 1 April 1918, the RAF inherited from its RFC and (especially) RNAS predecessors an overall total of 238 motor marine vessels of myriad types, shapes and sizes, and purposes — these being used mainly for attending to the routine needs of the Services' flying boats and floatplanes then in first- and second-line use. During the 1920s and 1930s progressive improvement in design of maritime vessels suited to the peculiar needs of the RAF — as opposed to the more generalised requirements of the Admiralty, for example — was relatively slow. However, by the mid-1930s the 37½ft Seaplane Tender and the 40ft Armoured Target Boat were entering RAF service, while in 1936 came the first 64ft 'Crash Boat' (*sic*) which was later retitled High Speed Launch (HSL). A further 16 HSLs were then ordered, though by the outbreak of war only nine HSLs were immediately available at UK or overseas bases — these few vessels in essence being the nucleus of the later Air-Sea Rescue Service.

By November 1939 the RAF's marine craft force was 'represented' at Air Ministry simply by the RAF Marine Craft Policy Committee, the Chairman of which was Air Cdre D. G. Donald DFC, AFC with 10 members and a secretary. Soon after, however a Directorate of Air Sea Rescue was to be formed incorporating marine craft and a mixed collection of 'spare' second-line aircraft, though in practice the RAF 'mariners' continued to serve various Command 'masters' in 1940-41. Finally, in August 1941 total executive control of all ASR operations was vested in the AOC-in-C, Coastal

117
A pair of 63ft long Type 2 'Whaleback' HSLs under way. No 122, first of its class, was based at Dover with 27 ASR Unit, and was sunk in the Dieppe operation on 19 August 1942. *PNA Ltd*

118
Throwing a lifeline to aircrew in their rubber
dinghy. *British Official*

119
The early pattern of air crew dinghy.

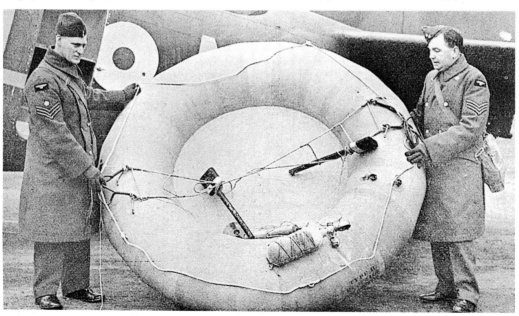

Command, at which time the Directorate of ASR was merged into the bigger Directorate-General of Aircraft Safety's aegis. The need for ASR services had been amply demonstrated throughout the Battle of Britain particularly, while its potential effectiveness could be shown by the period February to August 1941 alone; a period in which at least 444 of the known 1,280 air crew men who had ditched had been retrieved from the sea. In 1942 this proportion of successes rose to 1,016 of approximately 3,000 ditched crew men, while in 1943 the annual total of rescues was 1,684 men. By then numerous improvements in equipment had been introduced, and the ASR Service greatly expanded, both around Britain's coastal waters and in most overseas theatres of war. On 5 May 1943 came the first operational use of the airborne lifeboat to rescue a Halifax bomber crew ditched some 50 miles from the English coast; a form of retrieval later used successfully as far afield as the Bay of Biscay.

By the start of 1944 the ASRS possessed 32 marine craft units operating HSLs around UK

coasts alone, while abroad were further units upholding the high reputation of the Service in the Middle and Far East zones. The strength of the Service eventually rose to more than 300 vessels employed primarily on ASR duties, with twice that number utilised in support of flying boat squadrons and similar roles; the overall manning for this 'RAF Navy' being approximately 4,000 men. Throughout the war RAF marine craft were increasingly used for specific duties in many major land/sea operations. At Dunkirk in 1940, for example, Seaplane Tenders from RAF Calshot alone rescued some 500 soldiers from the besieged beaches; while on 6 June 1944 — D-Day — no less than 136 RAF marine vessels were deployed in the main assault areas off Normandy. In the overseas commands RAF 'sailors' took their craft deep into enemy-held waters on mercy missions or clandestine operations, and were in attendance off all the major Allied invasion beaches during the various Middle East campaigns. By August 1945 the ASRS had retrieved from UK waters totals of at least 3,723 RAF and 1,998 USAAF airmen, apart from some 500 enemy airmen, while in the overseas theatres a further minimum of 3,200 air crew men and 4,665 soldiers, sailors and civilians had been saved from a watery grave. The ASRS' motto — 'The Sea shall not have them' — had been exemplified in superb manner.

120
Refuelling Launch No 2072 about to tend her charge, Short Sunderland III, ML778, '2-S', of 422 Sqn RCAF at Pembroke Dock on 8 December 1944. This aircraft later became NS-Z of 201 Sqn RAF in 1945. *Public Archives of Canada*

RAF Awards and Badges

Most British gallantry decorations can be awarded to members of all three fighting Services, ie Royal Navy, Army and Royal Air Force, but each Service also reserves certain decorations for members of its own formations. The supreme British award for gallantry against a declared enemy of war is the Victoria Cross, originally instituted on 29 January 1856. Next in order of precedence are the George Cross and George Medal, instituted by HM King George VI on 24 September 1940, originally intended for civilians only but later made available to Servicemen and women. The Distinguished Service Order (DSO) is a Service award, either for individual acts of superb courage, leadership, or other forms of distinguished service, but is only awarded to commissioned officers of the three Services. Other nominally 'one-Service' awards which came to be 'shared', albeit relatively rarely, with the RAF include the Army's Military Cross (MC) and its equivalent Military Medal (MM) for non-commissioned airmen; and the naval Distinguished Service Cross (DSC) and Distinguished Service Medal (DSM).

Of the 'pure' RAF decorations, the highest in precedence is the Distinguished Flying Cross (DFC) awarded to commissioned and Warrant officers, and its 'other ranks' equivalent Distinguished Flying Medal (DFM) for non-commissioned personnel. Both awards were instituted by HM King George V on his 53rd birthday, 3 June 1918, and a total of 1,100 DFCs were granted between that date and 1919 to officers. The terms of 'reference' for recommending the award of a DFC and DFM was for exceptional courage, or devotion to duty, while flying on active operations against 'the enemy'. This latter phrase, normally associated with any declared state of war, was extended slightly later, and included the various, highly operational activities under-

taken by the RAF in several overseas areas and countries during 1918-39, and, indeed, since 1945. The original DFC award of 1918 had a ribbon of violet and white *horizontal* striping, but this was changed shortly after to the present *diagonal* violet/white striping. The total number of DFCs awarded to officers and warrant officers during 1939-45 amounted to 19,247. The DFM is literally a medal (as opposed to a cross), ie of oval-shaped design, and its ribbon, though similar in design and colours to the DFC, has narrower violet/white striping.

A rarer gallantry award of long institution is the Conspicuous Gallantry Medal (CGM), created initially solely for non-commissioned personnel serving in the Crimean War but reinstituted in 1874 for the Royal Navy and Royal Marines. In 1942 non-commissioned personnel of the RAF also became eligible, but its ribbon was slightly changed from the naval medal of white with dark blue edges to pale blue with dark blue edges. The CGM, in order of precedence superior to the DFM, was awarded for acts of conspicuous gallantry while engaged on active flying operations against 'the enemy'.

The Army's Military Cross (MC) and Military Medal (MM), originally instituted for officers in 1914 (MC) and non-commissioned personnel (MM) in 1916, were available to RAF personnel for acts of courage on active *ground* operations (as opposed to *flying* operations); many such awards being made to members of the RAF Regiment *et al* during 1939-45. The MC's riband comprises white, purple, white vertical striping of equal widths; while the riband of the MM consists of three white and two crimson vertical stripes, bordered by broad navy-blue edges.

Also instituted in 1918 were the Air Force Cross (AFC) and Air Force Medal (AFM), both

was indicated on normal ribbons on tunics by a small silver rosette metal badge sewn on the ribbon. Each Bar was held to be the full equivalent of an original award of the decoration involved.

In addition to pure gallantry awards, RAF and WAAF personnel generally became eligible for a number of Stars and Medals eventually issued in respect of the various campaigns and battles, etc, of the war, depending simply on individual qualifying service in the areas defined, eg North Africa Star, Atlantic Star, Burma Star, *et al*. In the main such medals were applicable to all three fighting Services and certain civilian organisations, but two were exclusive to the RAF — the Aircrew Europe Star, and the Clasp to the 1939-45 Star. The Aircrew Europe Star, instituted in early

122
Ace meets King. Flt Lt Geoffrey 'Sammy' Allard DFC, DFM, of 85 Sqn receives his DFC and a Bar to his DFM from his sovereign at Debden on 16 January 1941. *British Official*

121
Cpl 'Jock' Wallace, an air gunner with 50 Sqn, receives his DFM from the hands of HM King George VI at Lindholme.

for acts of courage and devotion to duty while flying, but *other* than for actual operations against an 'enemy'. Personnel often eligible for these awards included outstanding flying instructors, test pilots, etc, including, incidentally, civilians engaged officially on such duties. Often regarded as *peacetime* equivalents of the DFC and DFM respectively, the medal ribands for the AFC and AFM were of the same design in striping, except that the colours were red/white instead of violet/white.

Circumstances arising *subsequent* to the award of virtually all gallantry decorations, ie another act or acts of equal courage to that which led to the first award, were catered for in many instances by the award of a Bar to the original award, eg DFC and Bar, etc. Theoretically, there were no limits to the number of such Bars which might be granted; eg Wg Cdr (later Air Cdre) J. B. Tait received three Bars to his DSO, and a Bar to his DFC, all for wartime exploits. The actual Bar was displayed on the medal riband in formal dress, but

123
A 'neutral' American from Cow Creek, Texas, in RAF uniform, 1940.

124
Kiwi. Sgt D. G. E. Brown, RNZAF, from Auckland, in the cockpit of his Spitfire. *Sport & General*

1945, was awarded for a minimum two-months' operational flying over Europe between 3 September 1939 and 5 June 1944 (the day prior to the Allied invasion of Normandy), providing the wearer had already qualified by serving two months of the qualifying service for the 1939-45 Star. Those air crews already qualified for the Atlantic Star, eg Coastal Command crews, merely received an 'Air Crew Europe' Clasp to wear on the full riband of their Star instead of a separate Aircrew Europe Star decoration. The Clasp to the 1939-45 Star was more commonly termed the 'Battle of Britain' rosette, being awarded to all crews who flew fighter aircraft engaged in the Battle of Britain, between its official parameters of 10 July 1940 and 31 October 1940. The Clasp on the full riband of the 1939-45 Star was simply worded 'Battle of Britain', and was denoted on normal tunic medal ribbons by a small gilt silver rosette sewn at the ribbon centre.

Throughout the 1939-45 war only two gallantry decorations could be actually recommended and awarded posthumously — the Victoria Cross and a 'Mentioned in Despatches'. The latter was denoted by a small brass oak leaf, sewn on the tunic, at the end of other medal ribbons (if awarded singly), or sewn on a relevant campaign medal ribbon. Foreign (ie non-British) awards, honours, and decorations could, if receiving official consent, be worn, but such medal ribbons appeared on the tunic *after* all British awards, awards in relevant order of precedence. Equally, non--British RAF personnel placed awards of their individual countries before any British decorations in the tunic medal ribbons display.

Trade Badges
While all air crew trades and few ground trades have traditionally worn cloth or metal badges on uniform tunics to distinguish them from others, the overall policy of the RAF on such 'adornments' has always been one of modesty and strict restraint. This policy remained in force throughout the 1939-45 war, albeit with a few rare exceptions tolerated temporarily in the interests of good morale. At the outbreak of war only three air crew categories wore any form of distinguishing trade badge ie: pilot, Observer, and air gunner. The RAF pilot's 'wings' brevet, along with the Observer's half-winged 'O' badge, had their origins in the similar brevets awarded to qualified personnel of the Royal Flying Corps

from 1913-18. In December 1913 the Naval Wing of the RFC — retitled Royal Naval Air Service from July 1914 — became entitled to distinguish its pilots by a small gilt eagle attached to lower tunic sleeves above rank badges. This eagle representation was to be perpetuated by the RAF in post-1918 years in its various badges and tunic adornments, *et al*, despite the many firmly-believed legends that the original bird was an albatross, etc. Contemporary official documentation in Admiralty and War Office records confirm unequivocally that the bird was an eagle, and this has been perpetuated ever since by the RAF.

The Observer's 'Flying-O' half-wing brevet of the RFC remained in use by the RAF after 1918 to denote what later came to be called navigators until September 1942, when a new half-wing brevet, with an 'N' encircled by a laurel wreath with attached half-wing was introduced to denote the newly-titled trade of Navigator. Nevertheless, those air crew personnel who had qualified for the original 'O' badge prior to 3 September 1939 were permitted to continue wearing their badge, though fully qualified in the new navigator category. The third air crew member permitted to wear any distinguishing badge was the air gunner — or 'aerial gunner' as this category was officially titled when a metal winged brass bullet badge was introduced by AMO A.204 of 1923 worn on the upper right arm of airmen's tunics by suitably qualified non-commissioned personnel. Although thereby recognised as an air crew member, aerial gunners were not regular flying crew by trade, being mainly ground tradesmen who had voluntarily undertaken such duties in addition to their proper trade. This 'status' for aerial gunners was to last until an AMO, A.17 dated 19 January 1939, finally 'legalised' the trade as a fulltime flying trade. In December of the same year a further AMO, A.552 dated 12 December 1939, also introduced the half-wing 'AG' air crew badge for qualified air gunners. At that period, however, all would-be air gunners were required to qualify as wireless operators before being remustered to their new trade, and therefore, on qualification, were entitled to wear the traditional 'Wop's' cloth arm badge, usually nicknamed 'A fistful of lightning' — hence, they were then termed Wireless Operator/Air Gunners (Wop/AG). The rapidly expanding need for air gunners to man bombers etc soon led to many recruits being trained as 'straight AGs' ie: without the need for wireless training; this

125
Sqn Ldr Clive Caldwell DFC, OC 112 Sqn in North Africa, receives honorary Polish pilot's 'eagle' badge from one of his Polish subordinates on 10 February 1942. *IWM*

126
Wg Cdr Billy Drake, DSO, DFC wearing his American DFC award. *British Official*

latter air crew trade soon becoming a separate air crew category with its own badge.

A further air crew trade was introduced by AMO A.190/41 in March 1941, when ground tradesmen already fully qualified in the skilled Group 1 ground trade of Fitter II (Engines) became eligible to volunteer to become flight engineers on air crew duties for the new four-engined heavy bomber designs entering operational service then. Appropriate rank and pay rates were awarded to successful applicants, but, initially, it was understood by such volunteers that on completion of their operational flying duties they would revert to their basic ground trade again. During the following years further separate air crew categories — each with its esoretic flying badge — were introduced; including air signaller, radio observers, air bomber (or bomb-aimers as these were more usually termed), meteorological observers, etc. In each case, the distinguishing badge was an adaption of the air gunner's half-wing, with appropriate letters within the laurel wreath, eg RO, BA, etc. Traditionally, all such distinguishing air crew badges were of cloth, sewn on to the holder's tunic left breast, above any medal ribbons, and over the tunic pocket. One air crew badge, however, was a metal badge. This was the gilt eagle badge worn on the pocket flap by qualified crews of No 8 (Path Finder) Group of Bomber Command. The PFF came into being from 15 August 1942 and all members who satisfied certain trade and operational requirements were initially awarded a temporary PFF Badge while still flying on operations, then, once completing their tours of such flying duties, were awarded the PFF Badge permanently, being given a PFF Certificate to that effect, signed and therefore authorised by the commander of No 8 Group, AVM D. C. T. Bennett.

Although entirely unofficial in the pedantic 'book' sense, ie unauthorised by the RAF's official dress regulations, a number of additional badges began to be worn by certain air crew personnel as the war progressed. Numerically, the most-worn of these badges was a tiny gold caterpillar brooch, its eyes represented by rubies, denoting a member of the international Caterpillar Club. This association originated in the USA in 1922, primarily by a parachute-manufacturer, Leslie Irving. As a 'club' it had (has) no premises, no subscription charges, no official 'reunions', and membership is of one class only — life. Membership was (is)

127
Grp Capt Max Aitken DSO, DFC wearing the Czech War Cross and a Czech pilot's badge in honour of his command of 68 Squadron which included several Czech air crews.

exclusive to anyone (male and female, civilian or Serviceman/woman) who has saved his/her life in any form of aerial emergency by the use of an Irving parachute. Applicants have merely to provide authenticated witnessing documentation of such a descent to be qualified for enrolment, each such member then receiving a caterpillar brooch to wear permanently. By the close of the war, some 23,000 new 'Caterpillars' had been enrolled from Europe alone; only one of these being a woman, Cpl Felice Poser, WAAF. Several other unofficial 'clubs' sprang into temporary existence during the war years. The Goldfish Club, for example, was for personnel forced down into the sea while flying and subsequently retrieved; its membership badge being a small metal goldfish brooch worn on the tunic left breast pocket

128
Grp Capt R. M. Field wearing the ribbon and cross of the CBE awarded to him by the King on 16 January 1941 at Debden. *British Official*

flap. Another, the Late Arrivals Club, was initiated in the North African campaigns of 1941 for Allied air crews shot or forced down in enemy-held territory who evaded capture and literally walked back to the Allied lines; their badge being a metal winged flying boot.

Individual pride in particular air crew roles was often manifested in other ways, though mainly 'unofficial' as far as Service bureaucracy was concerned. For example, it became an accepted 'fashion' amongst fighter pilots, particularly during the early war years, to leave the top tunic button unfastened to denote their 'status' as distinct from other types of pilot in the RAF. Other external evidence of specific associations were the wearing of such badges as the Polish Air Force's pilot insigne above normal RAF 'wings'

by RAF pilots commanding units with expatriate Polish crews among their personnel. Other 'traditions' in dress for specific air crew roles might be exemplified by long-serving members of Coastal Command, whose tunic and cap buttons and badges soon became encrusted with green verdigris from long exposure to salt corrosion on maritime duties, but who refused to restore such items to normal highly-polished brilliance of 'parade ground' standards in order to proclaim silently their air-sea role. All such 'divergencies' from correct RAF dress regulations tended to be tolerated by 'higher authority' to some degree during the war years, but were quickly 'frowned upon' and eliminated once the RAF returned to peacetime after 1945.

If air crews were 'permitted' a certain 'flexibility' in matters of 'illegal' adornments and dress mannerisms, the non-flying ground tradesmen and women enjoyed little such 'laxity'. Beyond the few authorised badges of rank and occasional trade, the ground personnel were expected to adhere to King's Regulations in such matters. The few permitted badges, of long-standing prewar use, continued in use, eg wireless operators' arm badge, musicians' metal badges, and the traditional Aircraft Apprentices' metal arm badge of a four-bladed propeller inside a circle. The latter, uniquely, was the only official badge permitted to be *sewn* on the tunic, all others being fastened by loops-and-splitpin attachment. Nevertheless, a few new badges came into use during the war for specific specialised duties. One of the earliest was a cloth badge of an aerial bomb, flanked by the letters B and D, inside a laurel wreath, indicating personnel engaged in the hazardous 'trade' of Bomb Disposal. Another early badge was granted for crews of the RAF's Air Sea Rescue launches *et al*, which featured a launch and the capital letters ASR in its design. Another wartime addition to RAF uniform was the War Service Chevron; small inverted red cloth chevrons sewn on the lower sleeve of a tunic, *each chevron indicating that the wearer — applicable to all ranks — had completed one year's war service. Like many other temporary wartime innovations, these chevrons quickly ceased to be worn after the war.

The standard pattern of both officers' and airmen's RAF uniform remained unchanged throughout 1939-45, and non-commissioned airmen of all ranks from AC2 to Flight Sergeant at the start of hostilities were issued with two

129
Polish fighter pilots in normal RAF uniform, but with 'Poland' shoulder flashes, and Polish Air Force cap badges.

No 1 Service Dress uniforms ie: the open-necked, lapelled tunic with brass buttons and metal-buckled waist belt; one of which was usually reserved for formal and ceremonial occasions, and therefore referred to as 'Best Blue', while the second was used as normal working dress, usually covered by Service issue working overall or dustcoat. In early 1940 a number of airmen serving in France were issued with a blue-dyed version of the Army's battle-dress 'fighting' uniform on a trials basis, and this form of RAF uniform — officially titled No 2 Dress — soon became accepted by air and ground crews as normal working uniform. The RAF Regiment, on its formation, however, retained the Army khaki battle dress as standard, with RAF eagle shoulder patches, a cloth embroidered shoulder flash 'RAF REGIMENT', and RAF blue berets as headgear.

Embroidered shoulder flashes announcing the wearers' country of origin (ie non-British) became officially approved within weeks of the outbreak of war, eg: Canada, South Africa, New Zealand, USA, Jamaica, etc; later extended to include virtually every country participating in the Allied cause. Within the RAF, when sufficient expatriates of particular countries had become available to form complete 'national' units, eg: Free French, personnel wore their own country's distinctive uniforms; while members of the Royal Australian Air Force (RAAF) generally continued to wear the very dark blue distinctive RAAF uniform. Up until December 1941 when the USA declared war against the Axis powers, Americans who voluntarily enlisted in the RAF — mainly by joining the RCAF first — wore standard RAF uniform, embellished with USA shoulder patches, while the first all-American fighter squadron within the aegis of the RAF, No 71 Squadron which officially formed at Church Fenton on 19 September 1940, was titled 'Eagle Squadron', and its members wore an appropriate shoulder patch of the American Eagle flanked by the letters 'E' and 'S'; the first of three such Eagle squadrons formed by the RAF 1941-42. Even after 1942 many American air crews already serving in RAF squadrons, though legally transferred to the USAAF and wearing full USAAF uniform, continued by personal preference to serve with RAF operational units.

Airborne Armament

During the 1920s, when actioning a correspondence file at the Air Ministry, Hugh Trenchard, the RAF's first Chief of Air Staff, annotated the file's minute sheet with a terse yet succinct note;' The Royal Air Force EXISTS for armament'. This basic principle — indeed, this prime reason for maintaining *any* air force — was seldom evident in governmental policies in Britain during 1918-34, with the result that on the outbreak of war with Germany in September 1939 the bulk of RAF airborne armament was overtly obsolete, mostly dating in concept from 1918. The years 1939-45 saw rapid advances in certain facets of aircraft armament, albeit mainly as relatively hasty improvisations or adaptions of existing designs and ideas, and the RAF remained well behind its opponent Luftwaffe in terms of general modernity in such weaponry. Broadly speaking, all airborne armament used by the RAF then came under the generic headings of either Bombs or Guns, though each necessarily included a host of associated equipment for storage, transportation, loading, arming, functioning, maintaining, *et al*.

Guns

Throughout 1939-45 RAF operational aircraft utilised one or more of five main types of aircraft gun:
0.303in Vickers Gas-Operated (VGO, or 'K')
0.303in Lewis
0.303in Browning
0.50in Browning
20mm Hispano cannon

Larger calibre shell guns came into limited use for specialised roles from 1942 onwards, eg the 40mm Vickers 'S' cannons fitted to Hurricanes in the Middle East for anti-tank operations, and the 57mm 6pdr cannon fitted under the nose of a few Mosquito FXVIIIs of Coastal Command

for anti-shipping assaults. The search for more effective guns for bomber turrets to replace the standard 0.303in calibre Browning machine gun led to a specification, issued late in 1943, for a new rear turret design, incorporating twin 0.50in Brownings, and produced the Rose turret which entered squadron use on a small scale from late 1944. Equally, 20mm Hispano cannons were mooted for turret armament as early as 1940, only to be vetoed for further development by the aircraft production supremo, Lord Beaverbrook. By 1941, when this development programme was slowly resumed the delay resulted in no such 20mm-armed gun turret reaching the operational scene before the end of the war.

Ammunition

All calibres of RAF ammunition up to, but not

130
Sergeant air gunner and his VGO 0.303in machine gun in a Fairey Battle of No 300 (Polish) Squadron.

131
Twin 0.303in calibre Browning machine guns in the rear seat of a Westland Lysander of No 400 (AC) Sqn RCAF at Odiham in early 1941.
Public Archives of Canada

132
Boulton Paul Type E, Mk I power-operated gun turret in the tail of a Halifax, with its quadruple 0.303in Brownings defensive armament.

133
The port wing 20mm Hispano cannon installations of a Hurricane IIC, with appropriate Belt Feed Mechanisms (BFMs) ready to be linked to the main belts of 20mm shells.

including, 20mm were termed Small Arms Ammunition (SAA), and 20mm and larger calibres were officially termed shells. All ammunition for machine guns came within one or other of the following categories:

Ball
Incendiary
Tracer (Day and Night types)
HE (High Explosive)
SAP (Semi-Armour-Piercing)
AP (Armour-Piercing)

With the introduction of 20mm cannons to general use additional 'mixed' categories of 20mm shells were:

134
Winching up a 250lb GP/HE bomb to the underwing bomb carrier of Mosquito LR374 of 613 Sqn, Lasham. These particular winch-hoists were nicknamed 'hockey sticks' by the 'plumbers' who used them. *Flight*

HE/I (High Explosive/Incendiary)
SAP/I (Semi-Armour-Piercing/Incendiary)
AP/I (Armour-Piercing/Incendiary)

In the cases of the VGO and Lewis machine guns, ammunition was fed to the gun from spring-loaded, pre-tensioned circular metal drums affixed to the gun manually; whereas the Browning machine guns and 20mm cannons were 'fed' via long belts of linked cartridges or shells stowed in ammunition boxes. Due to the sheer weight of such ammunition belts being liable to overstrain the gun feed mechanisms, mechanical or power-assisted devices were placed at appropriate locations between ammunition supply boxes and the guns to literally assist the smooth flow of the belt towards the gun. For 20mm Hispano cannons a Belt Feed Mechanism (BFM), a simple encased multi-sprocket rotary 'assister', pre-tensioned by means of its powerful metal spring-coil, was attached to the cannon. All ammunition at that period relied on physical striking of a shell or cartridge's base percussion cap to ignite the propellant charge within each round of ammunition, which in turn propelled the bullet or shell through the barrel.

Bombs
Aircraft bombs during 1939-45 in RAF use were grouped into specific categories and classes, the largest group being High Explosive (HE). Within this latter group were various classes:

General Purpose (GP)
Armour-Piercing (AP)
Medium Capacity (MC)
High Capacity (HC)
Deep Penetration (DP)
Fragmentation

All HE bombs, even including the standard 20lb Fragmentation, were categorised basically according to gross weight and Charge/Weight Ratio (CWR). CWR was simply a figure giving the *percentage* of the stated gross weight which was pure explosive filling. In broad terms GP bombs all had a CWR of approximately 30-35%; MC bombs a CWR of approximately 40-50%; and HC bombs a CWR of roughly 75-80%.

Other groups of bombs included Incendiary, Practice, and the multi-varied category of all Pyrotechnics. Within the Incendiary group were the basic 4lb hexagonal 'stick' incendiary used to effectively, and virtually any or all other pure fire-raising forms of 'bomb', or 'store' (as the RAF termed them officially). The Pyrotechnic group was the most varied and extensive during the war years, including many devices for illumination, target-marking and identification stores, ranging in weight from a few pounds to such monster 'fireworks' as the 4,000lb 'Pink Pansy' and 'Red Spot Fire'. Pyrotechnics also included photographic flashes, flares, marine markers, smoke generators, sea markers, signal cartridges, and a dozen other mundane items used both in aircraft and on the ground in routine procedures.

High explosive bombs had as main fillings explosives generally insensitive to heat or shock, enabling such bombs to be handled safely in less than perfect circumstances. To initiate main fillings, HE bombs had a built-in intermediary pocket in nose and/or tail containing a mildly sensitive explosive; which in turn contained provision for a detonator to be inserted. Thus, a 'train' of explosives was completed, needing only the detonator to be struck physically in order to set off the 'train' and explode the bomb's main filling. Two main devices were needed to initiate this train, namely pistols or fuzes. A pistol was a purely mechanical device, screwed into the detonator pocket by hand, and containing a striker mechanism, but *no* explosive. A fuze, on the other hand, contained a small filling of highly sensitive explosive, and when used replaced the need for a detonator. Detonators were in various classifications. depending on what, if any, delay they incorporated before actually initiating the train of explosion. This delay ranged from zero (ie instantaneous on surface impact of the bomb) by stages to 25 seconds. Greater delays were catered for by a series of special bomb fuzes, offering delayed action of the bomb from six hours to seven days. Certain long-delay fuzes incorporated anti-removal devices, thereby preventing enemy bomb disposal squads from rendering such bombs 'safe' — though in practice such fuzes presented yet another hazard for RAF armourers should any bomb so fitted be brought back to base after an operational sortie for any reason.

Rocket Projectiles

The history of applying the principles of rocket propulsion to missiles stretches back in time for many centuries; indeed, such missiles are recorded as being used by French armies in the early part of the 19th century, among others. Though superseded by far more accurate

135
Lapping in the 0.303in cartridge belts of a 613 Sqn Mosquito nose armament. Note flash eliminator attachments on barrels of the Browning machine guns. *Flight*

136
Can-openers. Twin 40mm cannons fitted to a 6 Sqn Hurricane IID in Egypt, for anti-tank attacks.

artillery guns, revival of interest in 'rocket-propelled' weapons included their use on aircraft during the 1914-18 air war, and research continued into development of such weaponry during 1918-39 by various nations. By 1942 the RAF had introduced the 3in Rocket Projectile (RP) to operational use by aircraft, mainly in the air-to-surface role for attacking 'thick-skinned' ground targets eg: concrete gun emplacements, or for attacks against ships and submarines. Though carried on under-wing attachments, RP had several advantages, including absence of recoil, a low launching velocity, and an ability to be aimed fairly accurately. RP were cheap to produce, and had a high destructive effect.

A complete 'round' of RP comprised a rocket motor tube, of $3\frac{1}{4}$in diameter and $55\frac{1}{4}$in length, containing a single, 11lb cruciform 'stick' of cordite — the main propellant charge. This 'stick' incorporated a simple electrical igniter wired to long leads which protruded from the rear end of the motor tube. Behind the 'stick', inside the motor tube, was a venturi arrangement. Externally, simple plate tail 'fins' could be slotted in to the rear end of the motor tube, and suspension sleeves, clamped around the tube, permitted easy attachment of the RP to the fixed RP launching rails on the underwing of an aircraft. At the nose end of the motor tube a screw-thread was incorporated to receive

137
Sliding 3in Rocket Projectiles (RP) on to their wing rails on a Beaufighter of 404 Sqn RCAF, Coastal Command. The RP heads here are 60lb HE/SAP. *British Official*

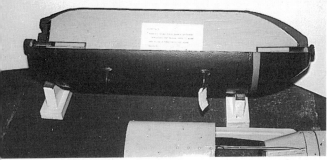

139
Sectioned 500lb MC/HE Mk 6 bomb, first introduced in 1944. Note built-in exploder 'pockets' at each end for intermediary explosive charge and accommodation for detonator(s), plus screw threading to accept pistols or fuzes.

140
PFF Mosquito being loaded with 250lb Yellow Target Indicators (TIs) at Coningsby. *Flight*

one of the variety of RP 'heads'. These included:

60lb Shell, HE/SAP
60lb Shell, HE/GP, Hollow Charge
18lb Shell, HE
25lb Shot, AP
25lb Head, Solid A/S (Anti-Submarine)
60lb Shell Practice, Concrete Head (Training only)
25lb Shot, Practice, Concrete (Training only)
12lb Head, Practice (Training only)

A normal RP 'battery' on RAF fighters com-prised four RP under *each* wing, these being launched in pairs (one from each wing in unison), or, if required, in salvo of all eight RP for a 'broadside' attack. Once the rocket motor's rear-protruding electrical leads had been plugged in to a mating socket in the air-craft's main electrical system, the RP were launched by the pilot using the appropriate switch in his cockpit, using the normal gyro gun sight for aiming purposes. In practice, pilots often had a line painted on the side of their canopy to line up with the horizon, en-abling them to apply the correct diving angle/ attitude for an RP attack.

141
Cookie. 4,000lb HC/HE blast bomb about to be
'digested' by Mosquito BIV, Srs II, DZ637 of 692 Sqn
PFF at Graveley in April 1944.
Hawker Siddeley Aviation

142
Tallboy. 12,000lb DP/HE bomb shackled into the
bomb bay of a 15 Sqn Lancaster, 1945.

RAF Commanders

BOWHILL, ACM Sir Frederick William

Born 1 September 1880 and educated at Blackheath School and in HMS *Worcester*. Became midshipman in RNR 1898, Sub-Lieutenant in 1904, Lieutenant in 1911. Gained RAC Pilot Certificate No 397 on 21 January 1913 and transferred to RFC (Naval Wing). Served throughout 1914-18 with RNAS, including command of aircraft-carrying *Empress* in 1914, units in Mesopotamia (now Iraq) in 1916, then air unit in East Africa, for which received DSO. 1918 appointed OC No 62 Wing, RAF, Aegean Group, and in 1919 awarded Bar to DSO and CMG, plus permanent commission as Wing Commander. Appointed Chief Staff Officer to Z-Force in Somaliland, and subsequently served in Egypt and Iraq. In 1929 appointed Director of Organisation at Air Ministry; then in May 1931 became AOC Fighting Area in the ADGB. 1933, appointed Air Member for Personnel, as an AVM, received CB in 1935, and knighted as KCB in 1936 with promotion to Air Marshal. Became AOC-in-C, Coastal Command on 18 August 1937, and remained in that post until 14 June 1941, when he was succeeded by ACM Sir P. Joubert. From 1941-43 he commanded Ferry Command, then became AOC-in-C, Transport Command until his retirement from the RAF in 1945.

BROOKE-POPHAM, ACM Sir (Henry) Robert M.

Born 18 September 1878. Educated Haileybury and Sandhurst, and commissioned in Oxfordshire Light Infantry, 1898. Qualified as pilot on 18 July 1911 (RAC Certificate No 108) as a Major, and following year joined Air Battalion, RE, then RFC in 1912. Became commander of an RFC Wing, 1914, served in France 1915-18, then appointed Brigadier-General, later Group Captain, 1918-19. In 1921 became first Commandant of RAF Staff College until 1926, AOC Fighting Area, ADGB, 1926-28, AOC Iraq Command, 1928-30, and then Commandant, Imperial Defence College, 1931-33. From 1933-35 he was AOC-in-C, Air Defence of Great Britain (ADGB); and from 1936-37 was Inspector General of the RAF. Retiring from the RAF, he was next appointed Governor and C-in-C of Kenya, 1937-39, but returned to service in 1939 and, in 1940-41, served as C-in-C, Far East, before reverting to the Retired List in 1942. Awards included GCVO, KCB, CB, CMG, DSO and AFC.

143
Sir Arthur Barratt.

108

CONINGHAM, AM Sir Arthur

Born in Brisbane on 19 January 1895. Educated at Wellington College, New Zealand, and joined New Zealand Army in August 1914, serving until 1916, when he transferred to the RFC for pilot training. In December 1916 joined No 32 Squadron RFC in France, and in next eight months was awarded DSO and MC for aerial fighting prowess. Wounded in combat, he returned to England for training duties, then in March 1918 formed, commanded and led No 92 Squadron in France until the Armistice, gaining a DFC. Served in Middle East 1923-26, awarded AFC, then became instructor at Cranwell College. Next served at CFS as Wing Commander, then in 1932 returned to Middle East for staff duties. In May 1935 posted to Coastal Area, and in January 1937 formed No 17 Group as Group Captain, followed by No 18 Group in 1938. In June 1939 appointed AOC of No 4 Group, Bomber Command as an Air Commodore, being awarded a CB in 1941 and promoted to Air Vice-Marshal to command No 204 Group in

144
Lord Douglas of Kirtleside. *IWM*

Middle East, from which the Desert Air Force derived. In January 1944, after receiving KCB knighthood and promotion to Air Marshal, became commander of newly-forming 2nd Tactical Air Force (TAF) preparing for the Allied invasion of France that year. From 1945-47 he was AOC-in-C Flying Training Command, but retired from service in 1947. On 29/30 January 1948 he was aboard the British South American Airways' Tudor IV, 'Star Tiger' airliner, G-AHNP, when it disappeared without trace between the Azores and Bermuda. Nicknamed 'Mary', a diminution of 'Maori' reflecting his New Zealand background in his youth.

DOWDING, ACM Sir Hugh Caswall Tremenheere

Born 24 April 1882. Educated Winchester and RMA, Woolwich, and joined Royal Artillery in 1900 until 1914. Qualified as pilot on 20 December 1913 (RAC Certificate No 711) and transferred to RFC in 1914. Commanded various squadrons 1914-18 in France, and awarded CB and CMG. In 1919 became Group Captain, commanding Nos 16, then 1 Groups, was promoted to Air Commodore and Chief Staff Officer, Inland Area in 1922, then served in Iraq. In 1926 appointed Director of Training at Air Ministry for three years, was again promoted and appointed AOC in Transjordan and Palestine in 1929. Commanded Fighter Area, ADGB, 1929-30, before becoming Air Member for Research and Development, 1930-36. On 14 July 1936 became first AOC-in-C, Fighter Command and remained in that appointment until 25 November 1940, being the chief architect of the RAF's ultimate victory in the 1940 Battle of Britain. Was Principal Air ADC to HM King George VI, 1937-43, but retired from RAF in 1942. He died on 15 February 1970.

FREEMAN, ACM Sir Wilfrid Rhodes

Born 18 July 1888. Educated at Eastbourne, Rugby and Sandhurst, and commissioned in Manchester Regiment in 1908. Gained RAC Pilot's Certificate No Fr.1404 on 21 July 1913, and transferred to RFC in April 1914. Served in France 1914-17, then commanded No 2 Training Group, South-East England in 1918. Awarded DSO and MC for war duties. By 1923 promoted to Group Captain, and in 1927 appointed Deputy-Director Operations & Intelligence, Air Ministry. 1929-33, Air Commodore, Chief Staff Officer, HQ Inland Area, then Commander HQ Transjordan and Palestine. Promoted AVM, 1933, and Commandant RAF Staff College in 1934-36. Next appointed Air Member for Research and Development in 1936, and helped progress production of Spitfire and Hurricane fighter aircraft, among others. Promoted Air Marshal in 1937, and ACM in 1940, be became Vice-Chief of the Air Staff, being knighted as KCB in 1937. From 1942-45 he remained Chief Executive to the Ministry of Aircraft Production.

HARRIS, ACM Sir Arthur Travers

Born 13 April 1892 at Cheltenham. Lived in Rhodesia and joined 1st Rhodesian Regiment in 1914. Returned to England 1915, obtained RAC Pilot Certificate No 2015 on 6 November 1915 and joined RFC. Served in France and England 1915-18, and granted permanent commission in RAF as Squadron Leader 1919. Served in India and Iraq, 1920-24, then commanded No 58 Squadron. 1927-29 attended Staff College, then posted to Egypt as Wing Commander on staff duties. Promoted to Group Captain, 1933, and Air Commodore, 1937, serving at Air Ministry until 1938. Next appointed AOC of No 4 Group, Bomber Command, in 1939 promoted to Air Vice-Marshal and posted to Palestine. On 11 September 1939 appointed AOC, No 5 Group, Bomber Command, until November 1940, when he was appointed Deputy Chief of Air Staff, with promotion to Air Marshal in 1941. On 22 February 1942, Harris became AOC-in-C, Bomber Command and remained in command until 14 September 1945. Promoted to Marshal of the RAF in 1945, and in same year retired from Service.

HILL, AM Roderic Maxwell

Born 1 March 1894 and educated at Bradfield and University College, London. Commissioned in Royal Fusiliers in December 1914 and served in France 1915. Transferred to RFC in February 1916, served with No 60 Squadron in France 1916-17, and awarded MC. Served at RAE, Farnborough 1917-23 and awarded AFC and Bar, interspersed with service in Iraq with No 45 Squadron, 1924-26. 1927-30 served at RAF Staff College, and 1930-32 was chief instructor to Oxford University Air Squadron. From 1936-38, as Air Commodore, was AOC Palestine, then became Director of Technical Development, Air Ministry with pro-

145
Sir Roderic Hill.

motion to Air Vice-Marshal, 1938-40, followed by period 1940-41 as Director-General of Research and Development: From 1942-43 he was Commandant of the RAF Staff College, and in 1943 was appointed AOC, No 12 Group, Fighter Command as an Air Marshal. On 15 November 1943 he became commander of Air Defence of Great Britain (the retitled Fighter Command from that date), and remained as AOC-in-C, Fighter Command when it regained its former title on 15 October 1944, until 14 May 1945. His next appointment was as Air Member for Training on the Air Council, 1945-46, followed by the post of Air Member for Technical Services, 1946-48, during which period he was knighted as a KCB and promoted to Air Chief Marshal. Retiring from the RAF in 1948, he died on 6 October 1954.

JOUBERT de la FERTE, AM Sir Philip Bennett

Born 21 May 1887 and educated at Harrow and RMA Woolwich. Served in Royal Field Artillery 1907-13, but obtained RAC Pilot Certificate No 280 on 3 September 1912 and transferred to RFC in 1913. During 1914-18 war saw active service in France, Egypt and Italy, being awarded CMG and DSO. Granted permanent commission as Wing Commander in 1919, promoted to Group Captain in 1922, and 1923-24 served at Air Ministry. From 1926-29 was instructor at Imperial Defence College, then received promotion to Air Commodore in 1929 and given command of No 23 Group HQ.

146
Top Brass. L-R: AVM G. B. Baker; Air Cdre A. H. Primrose; AVM J. M. Robb; AVM A. Durston; Air Cdre S. P. Simpson; ACM Sir P. Joubert; AVM G. R. Bromet; Air Cdre I. T. Lloyd; Air Cdre H. G. Smart. The occasion was a Group commanders' conference at Coastal Command HQ, Northwood in 1942.
British Official

In 1930 appointed Commandant, RAF Staff College, and in 1934, as Air Vice-Marshal, became AOC, HQ Inland Area. From 1936 — 1937 was AOC-in-C, Coastal Command as Air Marshal, then appointed AOC, India, 1937-39, being knighted as a KCB in 1938. In 1940-41 was in staff of CAS, then appointed AOC-in-C, Coastal Command from 14 June 1941 to 5 February 1943. Retiring from service in 1943, he was re-employed 1943-45 before finally retiring to become Director of Public Relations, Air Ministry, 1946-47.

LEIGH-MALLORY, ACM Sir Trafford

Born 11 July 1892 and educated at Haileybury and Cambridge. Joined Lancashire Fusiliers and served in France 1915, then transferred to RFC in 1916 and served in France 1917-18. Remained in RAF after the war, and by 1927 was Wing Commander Air Staff at No 22 Group HQ. From 1927-30 he commanded the School of Army Co-operation at Old Sarum, followed by two years as instructor at the Staff College, Camberley. By 1939 he had risen to Air Vice-Marshal, and was AOC, No 12 Group, Fighter Command. He remained in this appointment until taking over command of Fighter

147
Sir Trafford Leigh-Mallory. *IWM*

Command on 28 November 1942, as an Air Marshal. On 13 November 1943 the Allied Expeditionary Air Force (AEAF) came into being, with Leigh-Mallory, now Air Chief Marshal, as its overall commander, to prepare for the Allied invasion of Europe in the following year. On 14 November 1944, while flying en route to India to take up his latest appointment as commander of the India/Burma air forces, he was killed in a crash.

LONGMORE, ACM Sir Arthur Murray

Born 8 October 1885 and educated in HMS *Britannia*, Longmore was commissioned as a Sub-Lieutenant RN in 1904. Qualifying as a pilot on 25 April 1911 (RAC Certificate No 72), he joined the Naval Wing of the RFC in 1912, and commanded No 1 Squadron RNAS in France 1914-15. Saw extensive service thereafter in England and Aegean, receiving DSO. From 1923-25 served in Middle East, then appointed AOC, No 7 Group, Andover and remained as such until 1929, when he received promotion to Air Vice-Marshal on 1 January 1930 and became Commandant of the RAF College at Cranwell, a post he occupied until February 1933 when he succeeded to command of RAF Inland Area. On 1 October 1934 he took up command of Coastal Area, remaining as AOC-in-C when Coastal Command came into official being in 1936. From 1936-38 he commanded the Imperial Defence College, then on 1 July 1939 he became AOC-in-C Training Command, but on 13 May 1940 he arrived in Egypt as commander of RAF Middle East. From then until May 1941 he remained in the Middle East, and was then ordered home by the Prime Minister, Winston Churchill, and on 1 July 1941 was appointed Inspector-General of the RAF. He retired from RAF service in February 1942.

LUDLOW-HEWITT, ACM Sir Edgar Rainey

Born 9 June 1886 and educated at Radley College, Eastman's School and Sandhurst, he was commissioned in the Royal Irish Rifles, 1905-14. Qualifying as a pilot on 19 August 1914 (RAC Certificate No 887), he transferred to the RFC and saw active service in France 1915-18, receiving awards of CMG, DSO and MC. Granted a permanent commission as Wing Commander in 1919, he served at Air Ministry until becoming Commandant of RAF Staff College 1926-30. Awarded a CB in 1928, he was knighted KCB in 1933. From 1930-32 he was AOC Iraq Command, then served as Director of Operations & Intelligence 1933-35, followed by a tour of duty as AOC RAF India, 1935-37. On 12 September 1937, as Air Chief Marshal, he was appointed AOC-in-C Bomber Command until 3 April 1940, when he became Inspector-General of the RAF for the rest of the war, finally retiring from service in 1945.

NEWALL, MRAF Sir Cyril Louis Norton

Born 15 February 1886 and educated at

Bedford School and Sandhurst. Commissioned in Royal Warwickshire Regiment 1905 but transferred to 2nd K. E. O. Ghurkas, Indian Army in 1909. Whilst on leave in England qualified as pilot on 3 October 1911 (RAC Certificate No 144), then returned to India where he eventually helped form a central flying school until 1914. Returned to England, joined RFC, and saw distinguished service throughout the war, being awarded CMG, CBE, and an Albert Medal for personal valour. From 1919-22 he was Deputy Director of Personnel, Air Ministry, and in 1926 became Director of Operations and Intelligence, and Deputy Chief of the Air Staff. Promoted to Air Vice-Marshal in 1930, he commanded Middle East Command from 1931-34, followed by an appointment as Member of the Air Council for Supply and Organisation, 1935-37. In 1937 he was promoted to Air Chief Marshal and became Chief of the Air Staff, from September 1937 until October 1940, when he was appointed Governor-General of New Zealand (sworn in in February 1941) and received promotion to Marshal of the RAF, an Order of Merit, and in February 1941, the GCMG. He remained in this post until 1946.

PARK, ACM Sir Keith Rodney

Born 15 June 1892 and educated at Kings College, Auckland and Otago Boys High School, Dunedin, New Zealand. Served with New Zealand Field Artillery 1914-16, then transferred to RFC and joined No 48 Squadron in France in 1917. By 1918 Armistice had been

148
Sir Keith Park. *IWM*

awarded MC and Bar, DFC, and credited with 20 aerial combat victories. Remaining in the RAF, he commanded Nos 25 and 111 (Fighter) Squadrons in the 1920s, and by 1935 was a Group Captain. In 1938 he was promoted to Air Commodore and went to Fighter Command HQ as Senior Administration Staff Officer to Hugh Dowding, and became AOC of the key No 11 Group, Fighter Command. Throughout the 1940 Battle of Britain his brilliant strategy and tactical employment of his Group virtually ensured the RAF's ultimate victory over the Luftwaffe, but in December 1940 he was replaced in his command by Leigh-Mallory and posted to training duties. In 1942 he was appointed in command of Malta's air defences, where again his tactical handling laid the foundation for eventual success. From 1944 he served as AOC-in-C, Middle East until 1945, when he went to Burma to become commander of South-East Asia Command (SEAC). Knighted as a KBE in 1942, he received a GCB in 1946 on retirement as an Air Chief Marshal, and died on 6 February 1975.

PEIRSE, ACM Sir Richard Edmund Charles

Born 30 September 1892 and educated at Monkton Combe School, HMS *Conway*, and Kings College, London. Joined RNVR and qualified as a pilot on 22 April 1913 (RAC Certificate No 460), then transferred to RNAS. Served throughout war, receiving a DSO in 1915 and AFC in 1919. From 1920-33 he held various senior staff appointments, then served as AOC British Forces in Palestine and Transjordan until 1936. From 1937 to 1940 he was Deputy Chief of the Air Staff and a Member of the Air Council, then in 1940, Vice-Chief of the Air Staff, before being appointed AOC-in-C, Bomber Command from 5 October 1940 until 8 January 1942. From 1942-43 he was AOC-in-C, India, and from 1943-44, Allied Air C-in-C, SEAC. Retired from RAF in 1945. Knighted as KCB in 1940, and awarded CB in 1936.

PLAYFAIR, AM Sir Patrick Henry Lyon

Born 22 November 1889 and educated at Cheltenham and RMA Woolwich. Commissioned in Royal Field Artillery in 1910 and qualified as a pilot on 3 September 1912 (RAC Certificate No 283). Seconded to RFC in 1912 and served throughout war being awarded an MC in 1916. Granted permanent commission as Wing Commander RAF in 1919, and promoted

to Group Captain in 1923. In 1925 he was Chief Staff Officer at Coastal Area HQ, and three years later succeeded to the command of HQ Transjordan and Palestine. Promoted to Air Commodore in 1930, he went to India as Chief Staff Officer there, and was awarded a CB in 1931. The following year he assumed command of No 23 Group HQ, and in following year commanded the Wessex Area. He was promoted to Air Vice-Marshal in 1934 and awarded a CVO in 1935, and in 1936 became AOC No 3 Group, Bomber Command, followed by command of No 1 Group in 1938. In September 1939 he was appointed as commander of the Advanced Air Striking Force (AASF) in France, and in July 1940 he was knighted as a KBE, promoted to Air Marshal, and sent to India as AOC-in-C, serving in this capacity from 1940 until his retirement from the RAF in 1942. He died on 23 November 1974.

PORTAL, ACM Sir Charles Frederick Algernon

Born 21 May 1893 and educated at Winchester and Christchurch, Oxford. Joined Royal Engineers in August 1914 as dispatch rider, commissioned, then seconded to RFC as Observer. Qualified as a pilot on 9 March 1916 (RAC Certificate No 2543) and served on active operations 1916-18, being awarded DSO and MC in 1917, and Bar to DSO in 1918. Granted permanent commission as Squadron Leader in 1919. From 1920 to 1934 served on various staff appointments, and commanded No 7 Squadron (1927-30). In 1934 commanded RAF Aden, and in 1937 became Director of Organisation, Air Ministry. In February 1939, as Air Marshal, was appointed Air Member for Personnel. In March 1940 was knighted as a KCB and on 3 April that year became AOC-in-C, Bomber Command until 5 October 1940, when he was promoted to Air Chief Marshal and became Chief of the Air Staff. He remained as CAS until retirement in 1945. In 1946 was awarded OM and KG, and created 1st Viscount Portal of Hungerford, and elevated to Marshal of the RAF. He died on 22 April 1971.

DOUGLAS, ACM Sir (William) Sholto

Born 23 December 1893 and educated at Tonbridge School and Oxford. Commissioned in Royal Field Artillery in August 1914 and seconded to RFC in January 1915 as Observer. Qualified as pilot on 2 June 1915 (RAC Certificate No 1301) and served as commander

149
Sir John Slessor. *MOD(Air)*

SLESSOR, ACM Sir John Cotesworth

Born 3 June 1897 and educated at Haileybury. Qualified as pilot on 6 July 1915 (RAC Certificate No 1447), served with RFC, 1915-18 in France, Egypt and Sudan, and awarded MC in 1916. Served in India 1921-22, attended RAF Staff College 1924-25, and then commanded No 4 Squadron 1925-28. From 1928-30 was at Air Ministry on the Air Staff, and next became an instructor at the Staff College, Camberley from 1931-34. Returned to India, where he commanded No 3 Indian Wing 1935-37, being awarded a DSO. On return to England was appointed Director of Plans at the Air Ministry 1937-41, and was then appointed AOC of No 5 Group, Bomber Command from 12 May 1941 until 25 April 1942, as an Air Vice-Marshal. His next appointment was as Assistant Chief of the Air Staff until 5 February 1943 when he became AOC-in-C, Coastal Command, remaining in this role until 20 January 1944. For the remainder of the war he was Deputy C-in-C, Mediterranean Allied Air Forces. From 1945-47 he became Member of the Air Council for Personnel, with promotion to Air Chief Marshal in 1946. His honours included a knighthood (KCB) in 1943, and a CB in 1942.

of Nos 43 and 84 Squadrons 1916-18, gaining MC and DFC. Awarded permanent commission as Squadron Leader in 1920, and served in various staff appointments until 1928 when he took over command of RAF North Weald. From 1932-35 was instructor at the Imperial Defence College, then became Director of Staff Duties, Air Ministry in 1936. Two years later appointed Assistant Chief of the Air Staff, as an Air Vice-Marshal, and Deputy Chief of the Air Staff in 1940. On 25 November 1940 he succeeded Hugh Dowding as AOC-in-C, Fighter Command until 28 November 1942, then moved to Egypt as AOC-in-C, Middle East. On 20 January 1944 he became AOC-in-C, Coastal Command until 30 June 1945, and was next appointed Air C-in-C, British Air Forces of Occupation (BAFO), Germany from 1945-46. Promoted to Marshal of the RAF in 1946, he retired the following year. He died on 31 October 1969.

150
Lord Tedder of Glenguin. *Planet News Ltd*

Selected RAF Slang

Service slang, as in any other tight-knit 'family' community, is inevitably esoteric; a traditional mix of cynicism, fatalism, and 'twisted' humour, which in combination produces a language entirely its own. The following selection of the more common *contemporary* day-to-day RAF 'slanguage' of 1939-45 reflects that specific period, though certain expressions were used both previously and subsequently.

Apron Tarmac surround to a hangar.
Arrival An aircraft landing of barely adequate standard.
Bandit Enemy aircraft.
Beehive Bomber formation closely escorted by fighters.
Benders Knees. Hence, 'Get off your benders'.
Bind Both noun and verb to indicate some thing/one boring, depressing: eg a binder — one who constantly complains.
Black Error of judgment; usual phrase, 'putting up a black'.
Blackouts Issue WAAF knickers or 'pantees', ie winter-weight, navy blue underwear. (See also 'Passion-killers' and 'Twilights').
Blanket Drill Sleep; alt 'Horizontal Drill'.
Blood Wagon Ambulance. Also 'Meat Wagon'.
Bob, or Bobbing To 'creep' or 'crawl': ie to ingratiate oneself with higher authority.
Bod Person or 'body' actually present, as opposed to merely a name on a list.
Bogey Aircraft suspected as hostile.
Boob Mistake or error.
Bought it Killed or 'Missing'.
Brassed off Fed-up, miserable. Alt: 'Cheesed-off' and 'Hacked-off'. Occasionally 'Browned-off' for lesser degree of misery.
Brat More fully, 'Trenchard Brat', ie ex-aircraft apprentice or boy entrant.
Brolly Parachute.
Brown Job Any member of the Army (see 'Pongo').

Bumf, or Bumph All paperwork; from 'bum-fodder'.
Canteen Cowboy Airman who fancies himself as a ladies' man; alt 'NAAFI Romeo'.
Can Full responsibility, ie 'to carry the can', or take blame for any job or decision.
Chairborne Any desk-bound job or duty, ie non-airborne.
Cheese-cutter Airman's prewar peaked hat.
Chief or Chiefy Flight Sergeant.
Civvy Street Civilian life.
Close the hangar doors Stop talking shop.
Clueless Ignorant, without ideas or knowledge.
Clot Idiot, fool. Anal to clots in cream, ie 'thick'.
Dear-John Noun. Letter from unfaithful wife or girl-friend, announcing cessation of relationship.
Devil-dodger Padre or Chaplain; Alt 'God-botherer' and 'Bible-puncher'.
Dim Poor, dense, stupid. Used in various contexts, eg 'take a dim view', or 'he's as dim as a Toc-H lamp'.
Ditch To land on/in water; from 'In the Ditch' ie the English Channel.
Dog Originally, sausage, but often used to describe any aircraft or vehicle with poor performance.
Drill, The Correct method or procedure.
Drink, The Sea, or other expanse of water.
Duff Incorrect or false (see 'Gen').
Erk Any airman below rank of Corporal, but used generically for all non-commissioned ground tradesmen.
Fish-head Generic term for naval personnel.
Fizzer Disciplinary charge, ie 'put on a fizzer'.
Flannel Flattery, humbug, 'waffle'.
Flap Panic, alarm, disturbance, excitement
Fruit Salad Decorations, referring to medal ribbons.
Gash Spare, surplus.

115

Gen Information. 'Pukka gen', ie reliable, or 'duff gen' ie unreliable or incorrect.

Gestapo Service Police (see 'Snoop').

Get some in Addressed to those with less service time.

Glasshouse Penal detention centre.

Golden Eagle Day Pay Day, ie 'The golden eagle lays today'.

Goon Mindless oaf, from characters in contemporary Popeye strip cartoon. Later used by Allied prisoners of war for their German guards.

Gone for a Burton Dead or killed.

Gong Medal or decoration award.

Got his Crown Promoted to Flight Sergeant.

Griff Information. Alt to 'Gen'.

Groupie Group Captain.

Homework, a piece of Girlfriend.

Horizontal refreshment Sleep.

Horizontal PT Sexual activities (PT=Physical Training).

I/C In charge.

In Dock In sick quarters or hospital.

Irons Knife, fork and spoon eating utensils issued to all non-commissioned personnel.

Jankers Period of punishment resulting from disciplinary charges, comprising parades in full kit, fatigues, *et al*.

Jug Guardroom cell or detention room.

Joy Satisfaction, eg 'Did you get any joy with your application?'.

Kipper Fleet Coastal Command.

Kite Generic for all/any aircraft.

Line or Line-shoot Boastful exaggeration of one's own prowess or abilities, etc.

Line Book Written and witnessed record of 'lines shot' by members of mess or unit.

Long-distance gong The Long Service & Good Conduct Medal (LS&GC) awarded to non-commissioned personnel (mainly) after 18 completed years of satisfactory RAF service. Often termed the 'Rooti Medal' from prewar Indian derivation.

Mae West Life-preserver jacket worn over chest by flying personnel on operations etc in case of ditching in sea: from name of famous Hollywood film star of generous statistics.

Mod Modification, mostly relating to technical equipment.

Mothers' Meeting Any conference of senior officers.

Naffy Play on NAAFI (Navy, Army and Air Force Institute canteen and recreation building). Known as the 'Tank' to wartime Halton aircraft apprentices.

Oppo 'Opposite number', ie pal, friend, mate.

Orderly Dog Duty appropriate to rank, eg Orderly Officer/Sergeant/Corporal.

Old Man, The Commanding Officer.

On the Hooks On a disciplinary charge.

Panic Bowler Issue steel helmet.

Paper Factory Air Ministry, London.

Paraffin Pete Flying Control officer i/c flares for early forms of runway illumination by night, using goose-neck flares, etc.

Passion-killers Alternative to 'Blackouts'.

Penguin Any non-flying person; also 'Kiwi'.

Peri-track Tarmac roadway for aircraft and vehicles around perimeter of airfield runways' area.

Piece of Cake Any task accomplished easily, without bother or fuss; simple to do.

Pit Bed.

Plonk Generic 'surname' for lowest airman classifications of AC2 and AC1.

Plumber Originally any member of armament trades, but extended later to most ground technical tradesmen.

Pongo Any officer in the Army.

Popsie Female, usually young and attractive.

Prang Crash, wreck. Used as noun and verb.

Props Propeller cloth badge worn on each tunic sleeve by Leading Aircraftman (LAC).

Prune RAF legendary pilot, Pilot Officer Percy Prune, who served as supreme example of what *not* to do; applied to any unthinking air crew member flaunting the rules.

Pukka Old inter-Service term; true, correct, dependable.

Queen Bee Senior WAAF officer on any station or unit.

Rings Cloth badges of rank worn on lower sleeves of all officers' tunics.

Rock Ape Any member of RAF Regiment.

Rocket Severe reprimand from higher authority.

Ropey Poor, slack, careless, unreliable.

Scramble Emergency take-off at fastest possible speed.

Scrambled Egg Referring to gold trim on peaked hats of officers of Group Captain and higher ranks.Alt: 'Marmalade'.

Scraper Thinner centre 'ring' of Squadron Leader's badges of rank.

Scrub Forget it, don't bother, eliminate, cancel.

Snoop Service Policeman (see 'Gestapo'). In USAAF only, equivalent term was 'Snowdrop'.

Sparks Wireless tradesman, from cloth badge of trade worn on right tunic sleeve of qualified personnel.

Spawny Lucky.

Sprog Recruit, anyone fresh to his trade or category.

Square-bashing All forms of drill training on the station square, ie the tarmac area on all prewar stations intended for parades etc.

Swede Anyone from rural/rustic origins, or with 'country' dialect; yokel.

Stationmaster Officer in overall command of RAF station.

Stiffener A 'binder', moaner, grumbler, bore.

Stooge Assistant, general dogsbody; 'Joe Soap'.

Strip Reprimand from superior, usually 'to tear him off a strip'.

Sweeny Hair-cut to Service standards; from Sweeny Todd, the 'demon barber'.

Tapes NCOs' cloth chevrons of rank, worn on tunic sleeves.

Tate & Lyle Warrant Officers' badges of rank; resembled well-known golden syrup manufacturer's trademark.

Type General classification, eg 'he's a bad/good type'.

Twilights Lightweight issue WAAF knickers of lighter blue shade (see 'Blackouts' and 'Passion-killers').

U/S Unserviceable.

View All airmen took a 'view' of any thing, eg a 'dim view of Snoops'; a 'bright view of leave', etc.

Wad Cake or bun.

Wingco Wing Commander.

Wizard Great, very good, excellent, first-class.

Works & Bricks Air Ministry Works Directorate; alt 'Wonders and Blunders'.

RAF Personnel Awarded the Victoria Cross 1939-45

(Includes Commonwealth: ranks/decorations as contemporary)

Name	Sqn	Date of Action	Date of Award
Flg Off D. E. Garland	12	12 May 1940	11 June 1940
Sgt T. Gray	12	12 May 1940	11 June 1940
Flt Lt R. A. B. Learoyd	49	12 August 1940	20 August 1940
Flt Lt E. J. B. Nicolson	249	16 August 1940	15 November 1940
Sgt J. Hannah	83	15 September 1940	1 October 1940
Flg Off K. Campbell	22	6 April 1941	13 March 1942
Wg Cdr H. I. Edwards DFC	105	4 July 1941	22 July 1941
Sgt J. A. Ward RNZAF	75	7 July 1941	5 August 1941
Sqn Ldr A. S. K. Scarf	62	9 December 1941	21 June 1946
Sqn Ldr J. D. Nettleton	44	17 April 1942	28 April 1942
Flg Off L. T. Manser	50	30/31 May 1942	20 October 1942
Plt Off R. H. Middleton RAAF	149	28/29 November 1942	13 January 1943
Wg Cdr H. G. Malcolm	18	4 December 1942	27 April 1943
Sqn Ldr L. H. Trent DFC	487	3 May 1943	1 March 1946
Wg Cdr G. P. Gibson DSO DFC	617	16/17 May 1943	28 May 1943
Flg Off L. A. Trigg DFC, RNZAF	200	11 August 1943	2 November 1943
Flt Sgt A. L. Aaron DFM	218	12/13 August 1943	5 November 1943
Flt Lt W. Reid	61	3/4 November 1943	14 December 1943
Flg Off C. J. Barton	578	30/31 March 1944	27 June 1944
Sgt N. C. Jackson	106	26 April 1944	26 October 1945
Plt Off A. C. Mynarski RCAF	419	12/13 June 1944	11 October 1946
Flt Lt D. E. Hornell RCAF	162	24 June 1944	28 July 1944
Flg Off J. A. Cruickshank	210	17 July 1944	1 September 1944
Sqn Ldr I. W. Bazalgette DFC	635	4 August 1944	17 August 1945
Wg Cdr G. L. Cheshire DSO, DFC	617	Various	8 September 1944
Flt Lt D. S. A. Lord DFC	271	19 September 1944	13 November 1945
Sqn Ldr R. A. M. Palmer DFC	109	23 December 1944	23 March 1945
Flt Sgt G. Thompson	9	1 January 1945	20 February 1945
Capt E. Swales DFC, SAAF	582	23/24 February 1945	24 April 1945

Three other VCs awarded to airmen were Lt-Cdr E. Esmonde DSO, RN and Lt R. H. Gray DSC, RCNVR, both of the Fleet Air Arm; and Flt Lt W. E. Newton RAAF, the latter being the only Australian airman, serving in the RAAF *and* under sole RAAF aegis, to receive the supreme award for valour.

RAF Operational Code-names 1939-45

Abigail Bombing selected German towns to achieve maximum destruction, December 1940.

Acrobat Projected British advance Cyrenaica-Tripoli, 1942.

Anvil Allied invasion of southern France, 15 August 1944 (also, 'Dragoon').

Avalanche Allied invasion of Salerno, September 1943.

Balbo Large formation of enemy aircraft.

Battleaxe British operation to relieve Tobruk, June 1941.

Biting Allied raid on Bruneval, 27/28 February 1942.

Boozer Bomber crew warning device of detected enemy aircraft.

Bowler Air attack on Venice harbour shipping, 21 March 1945.

Cab Rank Patrolling fighter-bombers on instant call for tactical attacks.

Channel Stop Preventative operations for enemy shipping in Straits of Dover by day, 1941-42.

Chastise No 617 Squadron attack on Möhne/Eder/Sorpe dams, 16/17 May 1943, led by Wg Cdr G. P. Gibson.

Circus Bombers heavily escorted by fighters, by day, over German-held territory, 1941-*et al.*

Cork Pre-invasion air measures to deny access to English Channel by German shipping, June 1944.

Corona Radio countermeasures equipment, November 1943.

Crossbow Countermeasures against V1 flying bomb, 1944.

Diver Fieseler 103 (V1) robot flying bomb.

Dynamo Evacuation of Allied troops from Dunkirk, May/June 1940.

Earthquake Bomber raids on tactical targets in Burma, 1944-45.

Eureka Portable ground radio beacon.

Exodus Repatriation by air of Allied prisoners of war, April/May 1945.

Fido Fog Investigation & Dispersal Operation — petrol pipelines lit alongside bomber runways in fog conditions at selected airfields.

Flashlamp Bomber assaults on German coastal batteries pre-invasion, 5/6 June 1944.

Flower Fighter patrols over German nightfighter airfields.

Fuller Air measures to prevent escape of *Scharnhorst* and *Gneisenau* from Brest harbour, 1941-42.

Gardening Aerial 'sowing' of sea-mines in German waters.

Gomorrah RAF/USAAF air attacks on Hamburg 24 July to 3 August 1943.

Grand Slam 22,000lb HE/DP bomb designed by Barnes Wallis.

Haddock Operations by RAF against Italy from French airfields, June 1940.

Harpoon Convoy air protection, UK-Malta, June 1942.

Husky Allied invasion of Sicily 10/17 June 1943.

Hydra Raid on Peenemünde research centre, 17/18 June 1943.

Instep Air protection for Coastal Command aircraft over Bay of Biscay areas.

Mandrel Radio muffling of German early-warning systems.

Manna Air supply of food to Dutch population, April/May 1945.

Millennium 1,000 bomber raid on Cologne, 30/31 May 1942.

Mutton Long Aerial Mine (LAM) experiment against German night raiders over UK.

Mastiff Air Supply and Evacuation of Allied prisoners of war in SEAC, 1945.

Newhaven Form of visual ground-marking of bombing targets.

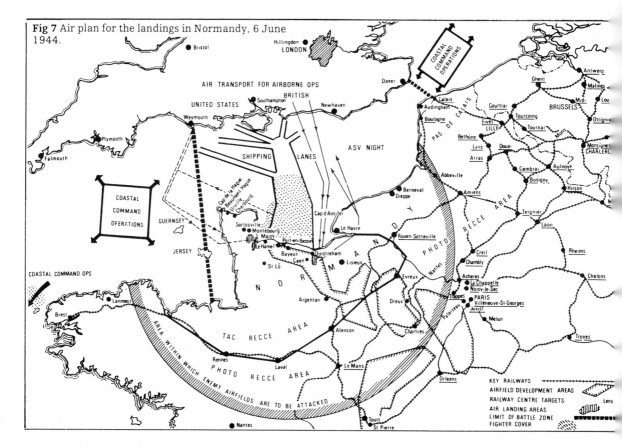

Fig 7 Air plan for the landings in Normandy, 6 June 1944.

Nickels Propaganda leaflets dropped by air.

Noball German rocket and flying bomb sites.

Oboe Blind bombing radar aid.

Pedestal Malta convoy operations, August 1942.

Pink Pansy 4,000lb Incendiary bomb used as target-marker.

Pointblank Bombing operations against German fighter force and its support industries.

Ramrod Fighter offensive sweep against specific targets.

Ranger Free-lance fighter intrusion operations.

Rhubarb General fighter sweeps to contain Luftwaffe in France, 1941 *et al*.

Roadstead Anti-shipping operations in coastal waters, 1941.

Rodeo Pure fighter sweep operations.

Ruffian German radio beam-transmitting installations, 1940.

Serrate Fighter's radar device which homed in on German aircraft radar.

Stopper Coastal Command operations off Brest.

Strangle Anti-Italian communications systems operations March/May 1944.

Tallboy 12,000lb HE/DP bomb designed by Barnes Wallis.

Taxable Aerial radar spoof operation over Allied invasion fleet, 6 June 1944.

Torch Allied invasion of French-controlled North Africa, November 1942.

Turbinlite RAF nightfighters fitted with nose searchlight.

Varsity Airborne operations supporting Rhine crossing, March 1945.

Walter Radar beacon fitted in dinghies for ASV-equipped search/rescue aircraft to home on.

Wanganui Blind sky-marking radar device in bombers.

Window Anti-radar strips of aluminium foil, dropped in air to confuse enemy radar detection devices.

120

Glossary of Common Abbreviations

A/A	Aircraft Apprentice
A&AEE	Aircraft & Armament Experimental Establishment (Boscombe Down)
AAF	Auxiliary Air Force
AASF	Advanced Air Striking Force
ACHGD	Aircrafthand, General Duties
ADGB	Air Defence of Great Britain
AG	Air Gunner
AHQ	Air Headquarters
AI	Airborne Interception (radar)
AMO	Air Ministry Order
AMWD	Air Ministry Works Directorate
AOC	Air Officer Commanding
AOC-in-C	Air Officer Commanding-in-Chief
AP	Air Publication: also Armour Piercing ref bombs/RP/SAA etc
ASR	Air Sea Rescue
ATC	Air Traffic Control: also, Air Training Corps
BD	Bomb Disposal
BEF	British Expeditionary Force
CB	Confined to Barracks. Punishment resulting from disciplinary charge(s), usually expressed in specific total of days
CC	Confined to Camp (see CB explanation)
CO	Commanding Officer. There was only *ONE* CO on any unit or station, ie the most senior rank appointed (see OC).
CTTB	Central Trade Test Board
CWR	Charge/Weight Ratio. Ref: percentage proportion of *actual* explosive filling of a bomb as against overall stated bomb weight
DZ	Dropping Zone
EA	Enemy aircraft
EFTS	Elementary Flying Training School
EO	Education Officer
ETA	Estimated Time of Arrival
EVT	Educational Vocation Training
FAA	Fleet Air Arm
FEAF	Far East Air Force
FLT	Flight (sub formation within a squadron or unit etc)
FTR	Failed to Return
FTS	Flying Training School
GP	General Purpose (type of bomb, of CWR 40% or less)
HC	High Capacity (type of bomb, or CWR 80% or more)
HCU	Heavy Conversion Unit, ie on to four-engined aircraft.
HE	High Explosive
HQ	Heaquarters
I/C	In Charge, eg Officer i/c Stores
IO	Intelligence Officer (colloquially, 'Spy')
ITW	Initial Training Wing
KRs and ACIs	King's Regulations and Air Council Instructions
LG	Landing Ground (hence, ALG=Advance LG)
MAFL	Manual of Air Force Law
MAP	Ministry of Aircraft Production
MC	Medium Capacity (type of bomb, CWR of 60% approx)
MO	Medical Officer
MT	Originally, Mechanical Transport; later, Motor Transport
MTB	Motor Torpedo Boat
MU	Maintenance Unit, ie base storage and/or major repair depot
NCO	Non-commissioned Officer. Strictly, Corporal only; SNCO=Senior NCO, ie Sergeant and Flight Sergeant
OC	Officer Commanding. An OC might be a senior officer commanding a Wing or Squadron, but might equally apply to a very junior officer given specific 'secondary duties', eg OC Station Pig Farm. *Not* same as CO.

OCTU	Officer Cadet Training Unit	
OTU	Operational Training Unit (air crews)	
PFF	Path Finder Force (No 8 Group, Bomber Command)	
PMRAFNS	Princess Mary's Royal Air Force Nursing Service	
POW	Prisoner of War	
PTI	Physical Training Instructor	
PR	Photographic Reconnaissance (hence, PRU=PR Unit)	
RAAF	Royal Australian Air Force	
RAE	Royal Aircraft Establishment (Farnborough)	
RAFVR	Royal Air Force Volunteer Reserve	
RCAF	Royal Canadian Air Force	
RDF	Radio Directional Finding (original cover-name for radar)	
RFC	Royal Flying Corps (1912-18 only)	
RNAS	Royal Naval Air Service (1914-18 only)	
RNZAF	Royal New Zealand Air Force	
RP	Rocket Projectile (ie airborne armament)	
R/T	Radio Telephony	
SAA	Small Arms Ammunition (generally, of less than 20mm calibre)	
SAAF	South African Air Force	
S Ad O	Senior Administration Officer	
SAP	Semi-Armour Piercing (bombs/SAA/RP etc)	
SASO	Senior Administration Staff Officer	
SHQ	Station Headquarters	
SOC	Struck off Charge	
SP	Service Police(man)	
SSQ	Station Sick Quarters	
SFTS	Service Flying Training School	
SWO	Station Warrant Officer	
TI	Target Indicator (airborne pyrotechnic stores)	
U/S	Unserviceable	

USAAF	United States Army Air Force (later, USAF)
VIC	Arrow-head formation of three aircraft or more
W/T	Wireless Telegraphy

Phonetic Alphabet

To ensure accurate transmission of messages (R/T etc) the RAF used the following 'alphabet'. Changes in the second column became necessary from 1943 when USAAF commenced full-scale operations.

Letter	1939-42	1943-45
A	Ac (Ack)	Able
B	Beer	Baker
C	Charlie	Charlie
D	Don	Dog
E	Edward	Easy
F	Freddie	Fox
G	George	George
H	Harry	How
I	Ink	Item
J	Johnny	Jig
K	King	King
L	London	Love
M	Monkey	Mike
N	Nuts	Nun
O	Orange	Oboe
P	Pip	Peter
Q	Queen	Queen
R	Robert	Roger
S	Sugar	Sugar
T	Toc	Tare
U	Uncle	Uncle
V	Vic	Victor
W	William	William
X	X-Ray	X-Ray
Y	Yorker	Yoke
Z	Zebra	Zebra

Selected Statistics and RAF 'Firsts'

Despite the lapse of years since 1945, finite statistics for certain facets of the RAF's war effort during 1939-45 are still impossible to produce; due mainly to a lack of co-relation among contemporary documents, particularly in the context of actual operational figures for such items as sorties flown, bomb tonnages dropped, *et al.* Nevertheless the following statistics may be regarded as the most accurate known to date, and at least minimums.

Personnel

Total strength, all ranks,
on 8 May 1945: 1,079,835
Peak strength, all ranks,
reached by 1 July 1944: 1,185,833
Peak strength of all ranks undergoing training,
in October 1941: 94,353

WAAF Strengths

Date	Officers	Airwomen	Totals
3/9/39	234	1,500	1,734
1/1/40	359	8,403	8,762
1/1/41	1,368	19,121	20,489
1/1/42	4,001	94,410	98,411
1/1/43	5,796	160,173	165,969
1/7/43*	5,974	175,861	181,835
1/1/44	6,040	170,780	176,820
1/1/45	6,355	159,810	166,165
1/5/45	6,278	151,008	157,286
1/1/46	4,373	93,371	97,744

Peak WAAF strength figures

Aircraft strengths

Total aircraft on RAF charge on 3/9/39: 10,208

Aircraft type strengths on 3/9/39
(All categories of state)

Bristol Blenheim:	1,089
Fairey Battle:	1,014
Avro Anson:	760
Miles Magister:	712
DH Tiger Moth:	583
Hawker Hart:	547
Hawker Audax:	425
Hawker Hurricane:	400
Gloster Gladiator:	396
Airspeed Oxford:	361
Supermarine Spitfire:	270
North American Harvard:	222
Handley Page Hampden:	212
Armstrong Whitworth Whitley:	196
Vickers Wellington:	175

Civil aircraft impressed into RAF,
1939-42: 1,017

Overall operational aircraft strengths

3/9/39:	1,911
1/8/40:	2,913
1/12/41:	4,287
1/3/43:	6,026
1/6/44:	8,339
1/1/45:	8,395

Casualties

Total RAF personnel casualties, 1939-45:

Air crews:	70,253	killed
	22,924	wounded
	13,115	prisoners of war
Ground crews:	9,671	killed
	4,490	prisoners of war*

3,253 of these in Far East theatres

Bomber Command

Casualties

Air crew killed on operations:	47,268*
Air crew killed, non-operational:	8,090
Aircraft lost on operations:	8,655
Total sorties flown (all types):	389,809
Air combat claims —	
Destroyed:	1,191
Probably Destroyed:	310
Damaged:	897

Includes — RAAF: 3,412
RCAF: 8,209
RNZAF: 1,433

Bomb tonnages dropped (3/9/39 to 8/5/45 only)

1939:	31
1940:	13,033
1941:	31,704
1942:	45,561
1943:	157,457
1944:	525,518
1945:	181,740
	955,044

Number of 12,000lb HE/DP 'Tallboy'
bombs dropped: 854
Number of 22,000lb HE/DP 'Grand Slam'
bombs dropped: 41*

By aircraft of 617 Squadron only

Strength of Command on 19 April 1945:

Squadrons: 97
Aircraft: 2,373

Fighter Command (inc ADGB)

Air crew killed on operations:	3,690
Air crew wounded:	1,215
Air crew made prisoner of war:	601
Combat victories claimed*	5,000+

(*as opposed to actually destroyed)*

V1 flying bombs destroyed by
RAF alone: 1,771*

638 of these by Tempest pilots alone)

Flying Training

Air crew personnel trained in the Empire (later titled, British Commonwealth) Air Training Scheme:

Canada:	137,739
Australia:	27,387
New Zealand:	5,609
Rhodesia	10,033
United Kingdom:	88,022
South Africa:	24,814
	293,604

By September 1943, when this scheme reached its peak of efforts, the RAF 'owned' a total of 333 flying training schools, as under:

United Kingdom:	153
Canada:	92
Australia:	26
South Africa:	25
Southern Rhodesia:	10
India:	9
New Zealand:	6
Middle East:	6
USA	5
Bahamas:	1

RAF/WAAF Ranks & Contemporary Abbreviations

RAF				WAAF	
			Prior to Jan 1940		*From Jan 1940*
AC2	Aircraftman 2nd Class	ACW2	Aircraftwoman 2nd Class	—	Aircraftwoman 2nd Class
AC1	Aircraftman 1st Class	ACW1	Aircraftwoman 1st Class	—	Aircraftwoman 1st Class
LAC	Leading Aircraftman	—	Nil	LACW	Leading Aircraftwoman
CPL	Corporal	ASL	Assistant Section Leader	CPL	Corporal
SGT	Sergeant	SL	Section Leader	SGT	Sergeant
F/SGT	Flight Sergeant	S/L	Senior Leader	F/SGT	Flight Sergeant
WO	Warrant Officer	—	Nil	WO	Warrant Officer
Commissioned Ranks					
P/O	Pilot Officer	CA	Company Assistant	A/S/O	Assistant Section Officer
F/O	Flying Officer	DCC	Deputy Company Commander	S/O	Section Officer
F/LT	Flight Lieutenant	CC	Company Commander	FLT/O	Flight Officer
S/L	Squadron Leader	SC	Senior Commandant	SQ/O	Squadron Officer
W/C	Wing Commander	CH/C	Chief Commandant	W/O	Wing Officer
G/C	Group Captain	CON	Controller	G/O	Group Officer
A/C	Air Commodore	—	Senior Controller	A/C	Air Commandant
AVM	Air Vice-Marshal	—	Nil	A/CC	Air Chief Commandant
AM	Air Marshal	—	Nil	—	Nil
ACM	Air Chief Marshal	—	Nil	—	Nil
MRAF	Marshal of the RAF	—	Nil	—	Nil

NB: Badges of ranks were the same for RAF and WAAF.

RAF 'FIRSTS', 1939-45

1939

September 3 First operational sortie by any RAF aircraft; Blenheim IV, N6215, 139 Sqn, photo-recce of Wilhelmshaven.

September 3/4 First leaflet (*Nickel*) raid on Germany; by Whitleys of 51 and 58 Sqns, on Hamburg, Bremen & Ruhr.

September 4 First RAF bombing raid of war; Blenheims of 110 and 107 Sqns attacked Schillig Roads, and Wellingtons of 9 and 149 Sqns attacked Brunsbüttel.

September 10 First RAF awards gazetted; DFCs to Flg Off A. McPherson, 139 Sqn and Flt Lt K. C. Doran, 110 Sqn.

September 20 First German aircraft claimed as shot down; by Sgt F. Letchford (AG) in Battle K9243, 88 Sqn, AASF (Bf109).

October 1/2 First RAF aircraft visit Berlin; three Whitleys, 10 Sqn, on 'Nickel' raid.

October 16 First German aircraft shot down in UK waters; two Ju88s of 1/KG30, by Spitfires of 602 and 603 Sqns.

October 30 First RAF fighter victory in France; Dornier 215, by Flt Off P. W. O. Mould, 1 Sqn.

November 18 First photo-recce sortie by Spitfire; Flt Lt M. V. Longbottom, from Seclin, France.

1940

January 30 First U-boat sunk by Coastal Command; U-55, by Sunderland Y/228 Sqn, shared with RN (scuttled by German crew).

February 25 First RCAF sqn arrived, at Old Sarum; No 110 Sqn (retitled No 400 Sqn on 1 March 1941).

March 11 First U-boat sunk by RAF unaided; U-31, by Blenheim IV, P4852, 82 Sqn, in Schillig Roads area.

April 4-8 First OTUs formed in Bomber Command (Nos 10-17 inc).

April 13/14 First mine-laying ('Gardening') sorties; Hampdens of 5 Group, off Danish coast.

May 7 First operational use of 2,000lb HE bomb; by Coastal Command Beaufort, nr Norderney.

May 12 Action by Battles of 12 Sqn against Maastricht bridges which resulted in later, posthumous awards of first two RAF VCs of war; to Flg Off D. Garland and Sgt T. Gray.

June 20 First RCAF fighter sqn (No 1), arrived at Middle Wallop.

July 1 First Polish bomber sqn (300), formed at Bramcote.

July 1/2 First Bomber Command operational use of 2,000lb HE/SAP bomb; dropped from Hampden L4070, 83 Sqn, on Kiel.

July 10 First Czech fighter sqn (310), formed at Duxford.

July 13 First Polish fighter sqn (302), formed at Leconfield.

July 22/23 First AI-assisted night victory over UK; Flg Off G. Ashfield, Blenheim, Fighter Interception Unit (FIU), Tangmere; Dornier off Sussex Coast.

August 2 First Short Stirling entered service; N3640 to 7 Sqn, Leeming.

August 25/26 First RAF bomb attack on Berlin; 81 aircraft from 3, 4 and 5 Groups, Bomber Command.

September 19 First American 'Eagle' fighter sqn (71), formed at Church Fenton (First sqn sorties, 5 February 1941).

November 10 First Avro Manchester entered service; L7279 to 207 Sqn at Waddington.

November 13 First Handley Page Halifax entered service; L9486 to 35 Sqn at Boscombe Down.

1941

January 10 First 'Circus' operation; six Blenheims, 114 Sqn, escorted by six fighter sqns, attacked Foret de Guines.

February 10/11 First Stirling operations; 7 Sqn against Rotterdam.

February 24/25 First Manchester operations; 207 Sqn against Brest.

March 1 First RNZAF fighter sqn in UK (485); formed at Driffield.

March 10/11 First Halifax operations; 35 Sqn against Le Havre.

April 1 First operational use of 4,000lb HE/HC ('Cookie') bomb; two Wellingtons, 9 and 149 Sqns, against Emden.

April 23 First RCAF bomber sqn formed in UK; 405 at Driffield.

May 7 First RAF Boeing B-17 Fortress unit formed; 90 Sqn at West Raynham.

July 8 First RAF B-17 operations; 90 Sqn against Wilhelmshaven (First B-17 operations ever in Europe).

July 21 First Norwegian fighter sqn formed; 331 at Catterick.

August 11/12 First RAF trial of 'GEE' radar aid; two Wellingtons, 115 Sqn against München Gladbach.

October 10 First Greek fighter sqn; 335 formed at Aqir, Egypt.

November 13 First Belgian fighter sqn; 350 formed at Valley.

November 15 First De Havilland Mosquito bomber entered service; W4064 to 105 Sqn, Swanton Morley.

November First Free French fighter sqn; 340 formed at Turnhouse.

December 24 First Avro Lancasters entered service; L7530, L7537, L7538 to 44 Sqn, Waddington.

1942

February 12 First Douglas Boston operations; 10 aircraft from 88 & 226 Sqns, in 'Channel Dash' operation.

March 10/11 First Lancaster bombing sorties; 44 Sqn against Essen.

April 8 First RAAF sqn in Fighter Command; 452 formed at Kirton-in-Lindsey.

May 30 First Mosquito fighter night victory; W4099, 157 Sqn (Sqn Ldr Ashfield) destroyed Dornier Do 217E south of Dover.

May 30/31 First '1,000-bomber' raid by Bomber Command, against Cologne.

May 31 First Mosquito sorties by Bomber Command; to Cologne.

June 3/4 First operational use of Leigh Light by Coastal Command; Wellington, 172 Sqn.

June 29 First USAAF 8th Air Force's operational sorties; by USAAF crew in 226 Sqn RAF Boston, against Hazebrouck.

September 18/19 First Path Finder Force (PFF) sorties; against Flensburg.

October 24 First *daylight* sorties against Italy by UK-based RAF bombers; Lancaster, 5 Group, against Milan.

November 3 First Lockheed Ventura operations; 21 Sqn against Dutch targets.

November 17 First Vultee Vengeance operational use by RAF; 82 Sqn, patrols of Bay of Bengal.

November 20 First Coastal Command Strike Wing operations; Beaufighters of 236 and 254 Sqns, North Coates, against enemy shipping.

December 20/21 First operational use of 'Oboe' radar aid; Mosquitos, 109 Sqn, against Lutterade.

1943

January 16/17 First use of 250lb TI (Target Indicating) bomb; by PFF against Berlin.

January 30 First *daylight* operations against Berlin; Mosquitos, 105 and 139 Sqns.

January 30/31 First operational use of H2S radar aid; 7 and 35 Sqns PFF, against Hamburg.

February 22 North American Mitchells first operations; 98 & 108 Sqns, against Terneuzen.

July 24/25 First operational use of 'Window' (anti-radar tinfoil); against Hamburg on first Operation 'Gomorrah' sorties.

September 15/16 First operational use of 12,000lb HE/HC bomb; 617 Sqn, against Dortmund-Ems Canal.

October 7/8 First operational uses of 'blind' 'G-H' (Mosquito, 139 Sqn, against Aachen), and 'Airborne Cigar' (ABC) electronic 'spoiler' device (Lancaster, 101 Sqn, against Stuttgart).

November 19/20 First emergency use of 'Fido'; four Halifaxes, 35 Sqn, landed in fog at Graveley.

1944

February 23/24 First Mosquito operations with 4,000lb HE/HC 'Cookie' bombs; 692 Sqn against Dusseldorf.

April 22 First Yugoslav fighter sqn; 352, formed at Benina, Libya.

June 8/9 First operational use of 12,000lb HE/DP 'Tallboy' bomb; Lancasters, 617 Sqn, against Saumur Tunnel.

July 27 First operational sortie by RAF's first-ever jet fighter Gloster Meteor, 616 Sqn (Fg Off McKenzie), from Manston.

1945

March 14 First operational use of 22,000lb HE/DP 'Grand Slam' bomb; Lancaster PD112, 617 Sqn (Sqn Ldr C. C. Calder), against Bielefeld Viaduct.

April 26 First Allied prisoners of war ferried by air to UK in Operation 'Exodus'.

Selected Bibliography

The following titles have been selected as providing *background* accounts of the RAF, 1939-45, deliberately omitting the plethora of individual biographical books published, with the exception of certain senior RAF commanders, but including a small section of 'classic' RAF humour books to provide rounded-out contemporary 'atmosphere'.

Air Ministry; *ABC of the RAF, 1941; Book of the WAAF, 1942; Women's Auxiliary Air Force (AP 3234), 1953; Air Support (AP 3235), 1955.*

Bishop, E; *The Guinea Pig Club;* Macmillan, 1963. *The Debt we Owe;* Longmans, 1969.

Bowyer, C; *History of the RAF;* Hamlyn/Bison, 1977. *Path Finders at War;* Ian Allan 1977. *For Valour — the Air VCs;* Kimber, 1978. *Guns in the Sky — Air Gunners;* Dent, 1979. *Coastal Command at War;* Ian Allan, 1979. *Fighter Command, 1936-68;* Dent, 1980. *Bomber Group at War;* Ian Allan, 1981. *Air War over Europe, 1939-45;* Kimber, 1981. *Encyclopaedia of British Military Aircraft;* Arms & Armour, 1982.

Bowyer, C and Shores, C. F.; *Desert Air Force at War;* Ian Allan, 1981.

Bowyer, M. J. F.; *No 2 Group, RAF;* Faber, 1974.

Brookes, A.; *Photo-Reconnaissance;* Ian Allan, 1975.

Collier, B.; *Defence of the United Kingdom;* HMSO, 1957. *Battle of the V-Weapons;* HMSO, 1964.

Dean, Sir M.; *RAF & Two World Wars;* Cassell, 1979.

Franks, N. L. R.; *The Greatest Air Battle (Dieppe);* Kimber, 1979. *Battle of the Airfields;* Kimber, 1982.

Hering, P. G.; *Customs & Traditions of RAF;* Gale & Polden, 1961.

HMSO; *Wings of the Pheonix,* 1946.

Hunt, L.; *Twenty-One Squadrons;* Garnstone Press, 1972.

Joubert, Sir P.; *The Forgotten Ones;* Hutchinson, 1961.

Lawrence, W. J.; *No 5 Bomber Group;* Faber & Faber, 1951.

Lloyd, H. P.; *Briefed to Attack;* Hodder & Stoughton, 1949.

Macmillan, N.; *RAF in the World War,* 4 Vols; Harrap 1942-45.

Mason, F.; *Battle over Britain;* McWhirters, 1969.

Moyes, P. J. R.; *Bomber Squadrons of RAF;* Macdonald, 1964.

Moyes, P./Goulding, J.; *RAF Bomber Command,* 2 Vols; Ian Allan, 1975-78.

Owen, R.; *Desert Air Force;* Hutchinson, 1948.

Pile, Sir F.; *Ack Ack;* Harrap, 1949.

Price, A. W.; *Instruments of Darkness;* Kimber, 1967. *Battle over the Reich;* Ian Allan, 1973. *Blitz over Britain;* Ian Allan, 1977.

RAF Cranwell; *Fifty Years of Cranwell;* RAF College, 1971.

RAF Regiment; *Short History of RAF Regiment;* RAFR Fund, 1974.

Robertson, B.; *The RAF;* Hale, 1978.

Saunders/Richards; *RAF 1939-45,* 3 Vols; HMSO, 1953-54.

Shores, C. F.; *Aces High;* Spearman, 1966. *Fighters over the Desert;* Spearman, 1969. *2nd Tactical Air Force;* Osprey, 1970. *Pictorial History of Mediterranean Air War,* 3 Vols; Ian Allan, 1972-74. *Fighters over Tunisia;* Spearman, 1975.

Smith, P. C.; *RAF Squadron Badges;* Balfour, 1976

Sprigg, T. S.; *The Royal Air Force;* Pitman, 1935.

Taylor, J. W. R.; *Pictorial History of RAF,* 3 Vols; Ian Allan 1968 and 1980.

Thetford, O.; *Aircraft of RAF since 1918;* Putnam, 1976.

Turner, M. and Bowyer, C.; *Aircraft in RAF service since 1918*; Hamlyn, 1981.

Webster and Frankland; *Strategic Air Offensive against Germany*, 4 Vols; HMSO, 1961.

Wood, D. and Dempster, D.; *The Narrow Margin*; Arrow, 1969.

Winfield, Dr R.; *The Sky belongs to Them*; Kimber, 1976.

Wykeham, Sir P.; *Fighter Command*; Putnam, 1960.

Biographies

Bennett, D. C. T.; *Pathfinder*; Muller, 1958.

Dodds, R. V.; *Air Command (Collishaw)*; Kimber, 1973.

Douglas, S.; *Years of Command*; Collins, 1966.

Harris, Sir A.; *Bomber Offensive;* Collins, 1947.

Hill, P.; *To Know the Sky*; Kimber, 1962.

Joubert, Sir P.; *Birds and Fishes*; Hutchinson, 1960.

Longmore, Sir A.; *From Sea to Sky*; Bles, 1946.

Slessor, Sir J.; *The Central Blue*; Cassell, 1956.

Tedder, Lord A.; *With Prejudice*; Cassell, 1966.

Wright, R. C.; *Dowding & the Battle of Britain*; Macdonald, 1969.

Humour, etc

Armstrong, A.; *Prangmere Mess*; Methuen, 1945.

'EBB'; *Winged Words*; Heinemann, 1941.

Marshall/Royce.; *Griff on the Gremlin*; Pilot Press, 1943.

Partridge, E.; *Dictionary of RAF Slang*; M. Joseph, 1945.

'RAFF'/Armstrong, A.; *Pilot Officer Prune's Progress*; Arandar, 1942. *Nice Types*; Methuen, 1943. *More Nice Types*; Methuen, 1944. *Goodbye Nice Types*; Methuen, 1946.

Raymond/Langdon; *Slipstream*; Eyre & Spottiswoode, 1946.

Thomas, S. E.; *RAF Parade*; J. England, 1944.

Ward-Jackson, C. H.; *It's a Piece of Cake*; Sylvan Press, 1943. *Airman's Song Book*; Sylvan Press, 1945.